人 文 與 社 會

第二輯　目錄

國家圖書館出版品預行編目資料

人文與社會 / 人文與社會編委會編. -- 初版 . --
臺北市：文史哲,民 91
面 ； 公分
ISBN 957-549-405-9 (第一冊：平裝) --
ISBN 957-549-491-1 (第一冊：平裝

1. 人文科學 – 論文, 講詞等

119.07   91023156

總 編 輯：劉仲冬
編輯委員：康家麗、董和銳、徐小梅
執行編輯：盧淑薰

人文與社會 (二)

主 編 者：國防大學國防醫學會人文及社會科學科編委會
出 版 者：文 史 哲 出 版 社
http://www.lapen.com.tw
登記證字號：行政院新聞局版臺業字五三三七號
發 行 人：彭　　正　　雄
發 行 所：文 史 哲 出 版 社
印 刷 者：文 史 哲 出 版 社
臺北市羅斯福路一段七十二巷四號
郵政劃撥帳號：一六一八○一七五
電話 886-2-23511028·傳真 886-2-23965656

實價新臺幣二六○元

中 華 民 國 九 十 一 年 十 二 月 初 版

護理關懷，關懷護理
（我所做過的護理研究及我所走過的路）

劉仲冬

國防醫學院

人文及社會科學科教授兼科主任

醫療與性別研討會講稿

謝謝大會給我這樣的機會，讓我能回顧我所做過的護理研究。其實不太好意思，我雖然很早開始針對護士做研究，但是在 1997 年之後就沒有發表過相關正式的學術論文，所以我今天報告的應當算是歷史古蹟了，給其他報告人做引言用。我的報告也許不學術，但是自忖是有生命的。

㈠醫療社會學護理研究階段（1976-89）

這個階段開始時我已經離開臨床，在一所護理專科學校教書。雖然放棄當時流行的傳統護理研究（如：如何護理什麼樣的病人），我研究的是護理人員及護理專業。因為自己當護生及護士的臨床經驗，讓我關心這個領域的未來，也關心從事這項工作的大多數女人的境遇。當時我運用我自己的護理經驗，努力想像外國的、本土的、傳統的、現代變遷中的護士角色，思考為什麼我們（或者我個人）扮演不好或扮演的不愉快。誰？或者怎麼樣才能調適得更好，扮演的更成功，等等。雖然我開始借用國外醫療社會的研究結果（當時護理專業還是醫療社會學研究的大宗，後來才轉向醫療），但是這樣的探討，老實說是沒有女性主義視觀的。我因為走上了醫療社會學的路，所以也推銷「護士何以應修習社會學」。在醫學院推銷社會學幾乎可以說是「此路不通」。醫學的視觀已經走到了分子裡面去，偏偏要討論另一個極端的超個人結構；醫學深信生物決定論，而社會學者非講授社會建構論不可，恐怕「不識相」或「不識時務」是最好的描述。

　　身為護理的一分子，我也曾大膽的建言「護理的未來」，我認為護理界都很上進，但是如果讓學生浪費時間跟在醫生後面跑，是不值得的，護理應當有自己的道路——照顧（care），所以課程設計也應當以行為科學為主。結果當然投稿被拒，退稿的評語是：「護理是一個專業，不容外人論斷」。評論人可能不知道醫療社會學裡護理研究的蓬勃現象，但是離開臨床護理工作就變成外人，或者專業刊物是否是一言堂，是否接受外稿？恐怕都得經過考驗。

　　也曾嚐試摸索用性別解釋護理難題，當時大眾醫學發表「男女角色的社會探討」（國防醫學院出版台灣的第一本通俗醫學刊物，持續三十年後停刊），更利用這樣的詮釋方式到某醫院演講，設法將婦運推銷到護理界去，記得當時一位臨床督導挑戰我：「如果像您這樣，優秀的女性都離開護理了，叫我們如何努力」。身為圈內人及圈外人，在研究上，有相當的好處及便利，但是也有吃裡扒外的罪惡感，及裡外不是人的尷尬。

　　㈡女性主義研究

　　(1) 1985-9是我重要的轉戾點，這段時間我在英國進修，寫論文。1989完成了博士論文：「白衣天使：台灣護士研究」。寫論文的過程一波三折。緣於我過去的訓練是量性實證研究的。我開始自護理流失的政策研究，終於很痛苦緩慢地轉折到女性主義研究：研究女性的主觀經驗及感受，也要知道她們如何看這些經驗及她們所生活的世界跟工作的環境。我開始將我的研究對象看成台灣女性。基本假設變成在每一件舉世通用大同小異的護士服裡面都有一個台灣女性，向外界張望著。她們有各自的生活經驗及感受，也有自己的看法。透過她們的描述，我想替這些女性的生命畫像。

　　台灣護士是站立在傳統與現代，東方與西方十字路口的女人。一個變遷社會的女孩在新興的西式醫療體系中，從事前所未有的工作，她們的角色是新的，經驗是獨特的，這樣的議題本身就很迷人。選到了好的題目，加上研究的路也是自省的過程。讓我朝思暮想，吃飯睡覺都在思考，所以順利寫完倒不成其為問題了。

　　當然為了替我的研究工作找尋歷史及社會定位，我搜尋了我國傳統的職業女性照顧者（三姑六婆），也對台灣的醫療體系做了功課。

　　研究方法是：女性主義視觀的質性田野研究及深度訪談。對人生的兩大選擇（女性的兩個生涯角色）：走入婚姻及工作的過程及經驗做了訪談，也用了部分的投射法及焦點團體，但是結果不理想，所以資料蒐集主要還是依靠深度訪談，一些「生活故事」的撰寫提供了對照。

研究發現：她們的婚姻及交異性朋友，並不像想像中的多采多姿（其實一般人對護士的像想是兩極的：乖乖牌及浪女），臨床的控制很嚴，自我設限也很多。這樣的結果受到挑戰：你的資料是不是太老了。

護士的臨床經驗，不外乎扮演女人，做女性的工作，被當做女人對待。她們對自己工作的看法也是女性的：愛護理，但不願為錢而做。她們期望被肯定，但是經驗是：「病人好了，感謝醫生。有脾氣，對護士發作」。對未來的生涯規劃大多走著瞧，視人生中間的重要他人而定，也就是父親、丈夫、兒子。這樣的態度加上臨床（包括護理專業本身）對年長者的歧視，當然只好走人。十年後我又在做了一次測試（不是同一批人，不能算追蹤），結果是工作時間延長了。但基本性質沒有改變。

這樣的結果受到各式批評：問題問的不對，資料是不是太舊了。樣本沒有代表性，研究方法沒聽過。

⑵軍訓護理課程：

我做軍訓護理研究是命運巧合，因為剛回來，不敢接質性研究的學生，怕口試不會通過。所以我幫忙一些軍訓護理老師做研究，因為這樣的機緣就接了這份衛生署及軍訓處委託的研究。

因為所有的女生都被想像成未來的照顧者，在戰場上也是「男生當戰士，女生當護士」，所以我們的女生都要上軍訓護理課。

我自己關懷的重點其實還是護理老師，訪談中的護理老師說：「軍護一體，他們是嘴我們是腿。有好的他們吃，出力的才有我們」。當時軍訓教官依官階升遷比照教職待遇支薪，她們沒有升遷（早期是有的，否則也不會找我做研究），但是值夜、上莒光課一樣少不了。

寫完了之後，除了陽明大學現任護理學院院長，當時的保健處長余玉梅教授，託人轉達欣賞之意以外，完全沒有得到任何注意，就像大多數的學術研究一樣，躺在圖書館一角落灰，等待也許有一天會有共同興趣的人青睞。

㈢ 婦運階段

三年後參加女學會，第一炮要攻擊的就是強化刻板印象的軍訓護理教育。因為有實徵資料，我的「軍訓護理」研究竟然上了報紙。隨著軍訓議題，我還上立法院發表「棄嬰、養女與陪嫁丫頭」一文。

　　在我的看法裡，護理老師就是護理界的棄嬰因為她們背棄了臨床護理或護理教學，貪圖教學的簡單，及不上夜班的安逸生活，跑去教軍訓護理，所以她們的情況沒有人關心。護理界本來就不喜歡太攻擊性，對自己本身的利益也不會太爭取，我這麼說可能有點刻薄，但是運動與學術不同，它需要簡單的概念及聳動的口號。軍訓處對待她們像養女，而立法院把她們當陪嫁丫頭，完全沒有討論就與軍訓一同送人情過關了。

　　當時軍訓處安排護理老師旁聽，我的語彙可能非常深沉的傷了她們的心。我當時希望她們自軍訓出走，我認為由於現代社會對健康及照顧知識的需求，學校裡的護理教育將來是有市場的。可是出走的路不簡單，很辛苦。其實我沒有跟護理老師面對面談過，她們對運動者有戒心，在那個時代，那種狀況下，是可以了解的。我自己上立法院也得冒很大的險，有一次幾乎以為自己會被「消失」。我記得那天獨自疲憊的從立法院走出來，心理感覺好落寞。

㈣我目前的關懷

　　因為婦運剛開始時人不多，所以幾乎所有有關婦女健康及醫療的議題，都分派給我做，因此我寫下了：女性醫療消費者、女性生殖與國家政策、代理孕母等等的文章。我不但被分派批判性教育，還自以為捨我其誰地跟生物決定論打對台……。這一切使得我的護理研究中斷，但是我對護理的關懷沒有改變，尤其是護理中的邊緣及弱勢者。

　　我最新的關懷是校護。刻板印象中校護是養老的工作，校護老太太只會擦擦紅藥水，其他什麼也不會。高雄市政府就將校護廢除，用醫院護士輪班支援。殊不知這樣的壞處有好多重，不但護理照顧將是片段的，校園將會被醫療化，而且校護是唯一護理人員可以做到退休的工作，現在反而因為校護不上夜班，不進步，是好缺往往有人情關說，而且退休金政府負擔重……就要廢除校護。這是典型的對女性工作的否定（女性工作是看不見的，不被肯定的，如：年長女性的經驗、與學生常時間建立的關係、親切、關心……都不算數），及對年長者的歧視。護理工作本來就沒有得到應當有的重視，校護更因為是年長女性受到雙重歧視。

參考資料：

我所做的護理研究：

1976 護生人格與其專業調適《護理雜誌》（57-61）

1980 護生之護理角色知覺（英文）《台灣大學社會學刊》（103-112）

1982`The Changing Role of Hospital Nurses in Taiwan' Essays on Medical Sociology

以下四篇蒐錄於（1991）《醫療社會學》合記：台北

1981 嬗變中的護理角色《德育青年》（p23-27）（119-127）

護士之角色（113-7）

我國護理的現況與未來（129-139）

護士何以應修習社會學（175-181）

（1989）Chinese women in White: A Study of Nurses in　Taiwan, (PhD thesis), Warwick
　　　University: Coventry, England

以下五篇蒐錄於 1998《女性醫療社會學》

（1990）護理論理的社會觀，《護理雜誌》，三十七卷，第四期，中華民國護理學會
　　　：台北

（1991）我國大專軍訓護理教育初探，《源遠學報》，第四期，國防醫學院：台北

（1994）我國的女性照顧者，《婦女研究通訊》，三十一期，台大婦女研究室：台北

（1996）護理人力的女性學解析，《台灣社會研究》，第二十二期，台北，p83

（1997）護理人力與護士女性化傾向間的關係

（1991）From San Gu Liu Po to `Nursing scholar': The Chinese nurse in perspective,
　　　Int. J. Nurs. Stud., Vol 28, No 4, Pergamon Press: Oxford, New York, seoul, Tokyo,
　　　pp315-324

台北監獄性侵害犯強制治療方案之需求與困境

李思賢

國防醫學院

人文及社會科學科助理教授

摘　　要

　　台灣社會近年來充斥著色情訊息，性侵害案件時有所聞，對於台灣婦女造成被害恐懼感，影響整體社會的治安。因此，立法院修訂刑法第16章，規定妨害風化各條之罪者，非經強制診療，不得假釋。由於性侵害強制診療法案已經推行八年，相關執行狀況卻相當缺乏，因此，本研究目的為描述監獄中執行性侵害再犯治療之現狀、困境與需求。

　　針對性侵害犯之訪談發現，參與治療團體之動機與意願大多是為了假釋，導致性侵害犯參與治療時有防衛心理及抗拒行為，甚至有合理化自我罪行的態度，將自己犯的錯怪罪於他人，與治療者拖時間，應付了事。但是，根據參與團體之性侵害犯表示，他們肯定強制治療，透過成員經驗分享，可以發現問題之所在，學習別人如何處理問題，治療後也發現較願意承認罪行，瞭解自己過去的錯誤行為，也比較會考慮到受害者的感受及後果。

　　治療人員表示目前仍以「再犯預防之認知行為療法」為主軸，目標是協助性侵害犯辨識及修正自己之認知感受行為鏈，學習自我內在管理及監督之方法，有效阻斷自己潛在之再犯循環，藉以防止再犯。治療人員遇到的困境或最擔憂的事情，一方面是治療評估是否通過會嚴重影響性侵害犯實際治療狀況，另一方面則是治療成效評估之標準為何？同時，治療人員也表示人力不足、治療環境差、治療時間不足、及女性診療人員擔心自我安危等是目前強制治療的困境。建議將在文中討論，研究結果可提供治療機構做為參考。

壹、前言

人有免於恐懼的基本權力，但近年來隨著性態度及性經驗開放（李思賢、趙育慧、黃沛銓、吳慶蘭、呂瑩純，2002），台灣社會的生活環境中充斥著色情訊息，人際關係日漸複雜化，導致性侵害案件層出不窮，大眾感到恐懼。性侵害犯罪狀況需要大家關心，因為性侵害案件不只對於被害者本身造成身心嚴重之傷害；另一方面，性侵害案件對於婦女所造成之被害恐懼感更是影響整個社會相當深遠。如何讓性侵害案件有效地減少，已經日漸急迫。因此，立法院為了保障個人自主權利意識以及預防性侵害犯假釋出獄後再犯罪，確實保護婦女安全，民國 83 年 1 月 18 日修正刑法第七十七條第三項條文「犯刑法第 16 章妨害風化各條之罪者，非經強制診療，不得假釋。」，希望台灣社會能夠免於性侵害的恐懼。由於性侵害強制診療法案已經推行八年，相關執行狀況的研究卻相當缺乏，因此，本研究目的為訪談台北監獄中之行政人員、性侵害受刑人、與團體治療診療者，探究目前執行性侵害再犯治療之現狀、困境與需求。

貳、文獻

性侵害犯是一個多重因素所決定的異質性團體，因此必須從多元整合觀點的角度探討，如社會文化、個人心理動力、生物醫學、家庭系統功能等因素來解釋性侵害犯罪。茲分述如下：

一、社會文化觀：Baron 和 Straus（1989）以犯罪社會學的觀點，討論強姦犯罪的理論，可分為以下四種（黃富源，民 84；侯崇文、周愫嫻等，民89）。

⑴性別歧視理論（Gender Inequality Theory）：此理論認為性侵害行為是性意識型態的偏見與歧視，在現存的父系社會，有利於強姦犯罪的產生；因為父系社會，會去刻意創造一個性別不平等的環境。而社會中對於女性的不平等，造成女性臣屬、附庸的次等地位，而強姦即扮演了父系社會中，實施社會控制的一種機轉，以維持這種不平等的狀況。此外，羅燦煐（民83）研究發現社會文化對於強姦犯的刻板印象扮演某種負面的功能，例如對強姦行為合理化、對受暴後果的淡化、對受暴婦女的責難、對受理的報案表示懷

疑、和對施暴男性的寬容。黃軍義和陳若璋（民 86）也研究發現：強暴迷
思、男尊女卑的觀念和兩性對立與強姦傾向關聯性很高，而且均達顯著水
準。換句話說，當個人的強暴迷思、男尊女卑、和兩性對立的觀念愈深時，
他就愈會有強暴的慾念。

　　(2)色情刊物論（Pornography）：此派論者認為情色傳媒對性暴力有正面
的煽惑與助長效果，使人縱慾性，濫交性伴侶，並刻意矮化女性、物化女
性、攻擊女性以強化男尊女卑的沙文主義。又可分為道德污染說和戕害女性
說兩類。Baron 和 Straus（1987）研究發現情色傳媒的發行量和強暴犯罪有顯
著的相關。

　　(3)社會解組論（Social Disorganization Theory）：持社會生態學（social
ecology）觀點的學者認為，在一個社會解組現象（高犯罪率、自殺率、心理
疾病率）愈嚴重的社會或環境中，該社會或社區，也就愈容易產生各種犯
罪。曾有學者研究指出，在離婚率和分居率愈高的地區，強暴犯罪比率也愈
高（Blau & Blau, 1982；Blau & Golden,1986；Smith & Bennett,1987）。此理
論也認為社會結構不平等的程度越高，男人與女人的暴力事件就越多，而這
也包括性侵害犯罪。

　　(4)暴力容許論（Legitimate Violence Theory）：一個讚許使用暴力，以追
求社會目標（如家庭教養、學校秩序或社會控制）的社會，會認定這種暴力
是一種「合法的暴力」，則此一社會，也就愈容易將這種暴力，轉化到這個
社會的其他生活層面裡。另外，性與暴力是特定團體成員內化的價值觀，是
他們社會角色與地位的表徵，也是他們生活的方式，以性做為人與人交往的
工具，利用性來得到好處，性攻擊是他們的普遍行為。

　　二、個人心理動力論：持此論點者大多認為性侵害者是孩童時期與父母
不愉快經驗，學習到偏差性行為，且缺乏社會技巧與適應力，形成不正常人
格特質或反社會行為。此理論解釋性侵害原因，性侵害者多出生於僵化、求
完美的家庭，往往有「不能失敗」的信念，也可能成長於不允許其表達情緒，
或較封閉的家庭中。在長大之後，由於生活單調無聊、困苦，他們對生活感
到不滿意、不快樂，因此尋求刺激性的活動，來滿足刺激的需求。或以遁入幻
想中（吸食迷幻劑、作白日夢、偷窺），以快速地逃離現實。Wolf（1984）亦
認為性侵害者由於早期有被虐待的經驗，學習不適當的行為方式，發展出不

良的自我形象及扭曲的認知系統，產生某種人格特質，在遇到壓力事件無法有效因應，性侵害者逐漸步入性侵害的循環模式（陳若璋，民90）。

三、生物神經醫學觀：此理論從生物神經醫學觀點解釋強姦犯罪，認為強姦行為與內分泌及神經系統的異常有關。例如攻擊性強暴犯男性荷爾蒙較高於非強暴犯，且使用暴力多寡與其體內睪丸激酮數量多寡成正比。研究發現性罪犯的左半腦明顯小於控制組，尤其是顳葉與額葉部份（周煌智等，民89）。

四、家庭系統理論：家庭系統理論（theory of family system）指出家庭功能是否健全與性偏差有關，諸如父母親婚姻關係發生變化，性功能或性關係失衡、挫折等，皆易導致性侵害事件，尤其父親侵害女兒的亂倫事件（侯崇文、周愫嫻，民89）。此外，家庭動力論（family dynamics theory）解釋如果個人擁有一個病態的家庭，使其親子管教與當事人學習的過程有所瑕疵，將導致其不良的社會化，終致促成強姦犯罪的發生（黃富源等，民88）。

五、情境因素：許春金、馬傳鎮（民88）調查台灣地區性侵害犯罪狀況與型態指出：對被害人之質化訪談發現，在案發之前，性侵害犯與被害者皆處於正常的互動關係。然而，隨著情境之改變，增加了被害者之弱勢，性侵害犯遂浮現性滿足的動機。而案發前飲酒，往往是加害者犯罪的重要誘因。此外，Marshall（1988）研究發現強姦犯在從事強暴行為之前，曾經頻繁觀看情色傳媒，因此他認為情色傳媒對強暴犯的犯行，可能扮演一種催化作用。

綜合上述理論得知，性侵害犯罪成因至為複雜，非單一理論可解釋，遂有理論整合解釋較為周延。黃軍義（民89）從社會文化、個人心理、情境與個人行為層次等四個面向，建構強姦犯罪之心理歷程的理論。在社會文化層次上，華人社會是以「男性繼嗣」、「男性為尊」的父權體制社會，在此文化背景下，出現社會多數是男性強姦女性的現象。在個人心理層次上，強姦者的認知、情緒、動機、經驗、意圖與人格，均對其強姦行為的形成具有影響。在情境層次上，強姦者會考慮當時情境的安全性、隱密性及風險性，而決定是否採取行動。在個人行為層次上，強姦行為的取決於個人的強姦意圖、人格特質與當時情境這三項因素間的交互作用。

參、研究結果

　　本研究為瞭解治療實施過程，獲得台北監獄的行政協助，與治療人員及性侵害犯同意後，以觀察者角色，探討治療者與成員互動情形，並依據觀察所得，擬定「性侵害犯強制治療訪談大綱（附錄一）」，包括治療處遇的內容、監獄組織氣氛、方案執行的資源等，並進行開放式的面對面訪談，主題與內容以受訪者的角度來談論性侵害犯的治療需求、治療所面臨的困難以及性侵害犯所感受到的治療效果。本研究綜列受治療者對強制治療的態度與感受，並且敘述治療師及行政人員對強制治療的各種看法。

一、受治療者訪談結果

　　研究者從性侵害治療團體中採隨機訪談 8 名性侵害犯，其基本資料如表一，以了解性侵害犯對於強制治療的看法，接受治療的動機，成員參與團體治療過程的感受。如表二，訪談結果可分為參與團體治療的態度、團體治療對成員的助益、場舍同學對成員接受治療的看法與成員治療前與治療後的差異。最後詢問其對治療課程有何建議及出監後再犯可能性。茲逐項說明如下：

　　1.受訪者基本資料：受訪者中刑期最短為二年七月，最長為十六年，犯罪類型以強姦居多，年齡從 19 歲至 57 歲，學歷小學 3 位，國中 2 位，高中 1 位，大學 2 位。

表一、性侵害受刑人基本資料

特性 編號	罪　名	刑期	犯罪類型	年齡	學歷
A	妨害性自主	三年	強制性交	28	高中肄業
B	強劫強姦	十六年	強姦	32	大學肄業
C	妨害性自主	三年六月	強制猥褻	57	小學畢業
D	強姦	八年五月二日	強姦	37	大學肄業
E	妨害性自主	七年	強制性交	32	小學畢業
F	妨害性自主	二年七月	強制性交	19	國中畢業
G	妨害風化	十二年四月	強姦	47	國中畢業
H	強姦	八年六月	強姦	44	小學肄業

　　2.參與強制治療的動機：受治療者有意願改變的動機是決定治療成功的重要因素，根據受治療者表示，多數參與治療的動機為提早假釋出獄，若不接受治療，只得服滿刑期出獄。因此以附加條件假釋，迫使性侵害犯接受矯治，易使受治療者忽視了治療的本質，而以治療為爭取假釋的手段，治療成效大打折扣。

　　3.參與團體治療的態度：在法律強制治療的過程，除了少數受治療者抱著有心改過，而願意探索自己的問題，其餘則顧慮監獄特殊環境，時有防衛心理及抗拒行為出現。如自認無病不需治療；只談些無助治療的話題；不願為自己的行為負責；將自己所犯的錯誤怪罪於他人；與治療者玩時間遊戲，應付了事等。

　　4.團體治療對成員的助益：雖然受治療者的參與動機和防衛態度影響他們在團體中的表現，但多數參與治療者對於團體治療仍抱持肯定；受治療者認為透過成員經驗的分享，可以協助成員發現彼此問題所在，吸取他人優缺點，建立回饋機制，更可進一步學習到解決自我內在問題的能力。

　　5.場舍同學如何看待受治療者：性侵害犯在受刑人的地位中屬於最弱勢的一群，受治療者最擔心被貼標籤，被場舍的同學以歧視眼光看待，或在背後閒言閒語。嚴重的話，以找麻煩的方式藉機修理或譏笑，因而造成受治療者對治療的排斥感。

表二、性侵害犯訪談內容摘要

參與治療的動機	
1.為假釋治療	F：我等待上課等很久了，進來快一年我才去治療，上完課就可辦假釋
	H：如果我們沒有上課的話就不能報假釋，大家為了都要報假釋每個人都要來治療，沒有人不願意來。
2.意識有病而接受治療	D：像我在診療的時候，我就跟老師講不論能不能通過治療，我希望自己可以在診療的過程中，真的學到一些東西，去看自己過去的罪刑。
	G：我覺得有需要治療，我會再思考過去怎樣，辦這個真的不錯！因為人生有一句話要覺醒啦，覺醒就不會再犯了呀，假如你不覺醒，出去還是一樣再犯啦！
參與團體治療的態度	
1.抗拒、逃避態度	A：了不起關滿刑期，治療通過與否，沒有影響。

	B：有些同學不願意來，是因爲心沒有放下來，可能本身會有排斥，不可能把他的內心世界完全告訴你，就無法把心事透露出來。
	E：我們團體有 12 個人，有眞心想接受治療的人沒有幾個，大部分的人都在說謊，對於自己的案情，都沒有坦白。
2.抱著好玩心態	F：我覺得上課很無聊，上課時聽不下去，就在玩。
團體治療對成員的助益 *1.敞開心胸，觀照自己*	B：爲自己以前所爲感到悲哀，現在學習讓自己的心放寬一點。
	F：幫助你，讓你不會想再犯罪！我是覺得自己現在比較會想耶，在這裡感覺還不錯，防止你再犯啦。
2.獲得知識，解決問題	D：我覺得觀念改變很多。團療教導一些方法，幫助我們趕快轉移心思。
	H：對這方面比較有認識呀……會清楚什麼是該做，什麼是不應該做的！
3.從聽取別人的經驗中　　得到反省	E：在上課的過程中，我從別人的身上看到自己的缺點，他們以前的缺點，在自己身上也發生過，其實這是最大的幫助。
場舍同學如何看待受治療者 *1.歧視、冷嘲熱諷*	A：人家會諷刺他，犯什麼罪要治療？
	C：他們的反應是不好的，他們說你什麼案子都可以，就是對妨害性自主方面比較氣。他們說你喜歡就去花錢，何必去強迫人家……。
2.找麻煩、欺侮	C：監所是團體生活，就會認爲你是故意的，故意找碴，找快出獄的同學跟你打架。
	D：把自己弄得跟刺蝟一樣，人家要欺負我，也會考慮一下。
治療前、後的差異 *1.情感的釋放*	A：我上完課後覺得心境很開朗，如果我把我的問題都講出來，那我心理的負擔就減少了。
	F：就是心裡沒有那種沈重，沒有那種壓力。
2.認知的轉變	C：事情會想的比較遠，都會考慮到對方。
	D：觀念上改變很多，感覺上差別很大。
	F：要怎麼講，就是感覺比較好就對了，比較會想一點，就是幹嘛會犯這個案子。

6.治療前、後差異：受治療者表示在治療前，心情沉重、抑鬱，有罪惡感，無法釋懷。經由治療師教導，成員瞭解過去的錯誤行為，開放心靈、舒解胸中鬱悶，凡事會考慮到對方的感受及後果。受治療者表示在治療後有負面情感的釋放，及對犯罪認知的轉變，對治療有正面的評價。但是，受治療者是否只是因為這次面訪而做這樣的敘述，不得而知。

二、治療師及行政人員訪談結果

表三是受訪治療師及行政人員基本資料，針對治療人員及行政人員進行訪談，以深入了解其採取何種治療模式、治療效能的評估方式、影響治療成效的因素、治療性侵害犯的困難等看法，並以表四呈現各種看法。

1.受訪者基本資料：本研究訪談治療人員有心理師二名，職能治療師與護理師各一名，行政人員以承辦治療業務的教誨師，及直接管理性侵害犯的戒護管理員。

表三、行政人員及診療者基本資料

特性	性別	職稱	教育背景	工作	專長
A	男	心理師	行為醫學所碩士	3 年	臨床心理
B	男	護理師	護理學院學士	7 年	精神科護理
C	女	職能治療師	職能治療研究所	9 年	職能治療
D	男	主任	心研所碩士	20 年	臨床心理
E	男	教誨師	大學學士	8 年	教誨教育
F	男	管理員	高工	11 年	戒護管理

2.治療模式與內容：目前性侵害犯心理治療技術，仍以「再犯預防之認知行為療法」為主軸，其治療目標是協助性侵害犯辨識及修正自己之認知感受行為鏈，學習自我內在管理及監督之方法，有效阻斷自己潛在之再犯循環，藉以防止再犯。此外，治療者會考慮此次團體成員的基本資料，例如，犯罪的手法、及犯罪心態等等，依不同犯罪類型組別，設計適合的方案，施予社交技巧、情緒管理等課程，對於再犯的可能性加以處理。

3.評估受治療者成效：受治療者最擔憂治療評估是否通過而合於提報假釋，因此，「治療成效評估之標準為何？」受治療者常感疑慮與不解。治療者對性侵害犯評估治療成效的標準係依據團體設定的目標，在團體中的表現，被害者同理心的培養及自我覺察等方面進行評定，然而，目前並沒有一套較客觀的標準或測量，僅能依賴治療者主觀上對於團體進行的品質評定。

表四、治療及行政人員訪談內容結果

治療模式與內容	
1. 再犯預防之認知行為療法	A：治療是以再犯預防的模式，以自我覺察的方式，避免受治療者再次犯罪。到底是怎樣形成這樣的一個犯罪意念，然後去找出犯罪循環，是什麼樣的原因造成什麼樣的犯罪。
	B：團體中個案犯罪動力都不一樣，大部分都是強暴迷思，或是認知扭曲，我們在團體中大多是做這方面的澄清。
	C：我們是採用認知行為治療的方法。
	E：治療者告訴你為什麼需要治療，本身有什麼問題，讓你知道犯罪循環，告訴你如何診斷，並透過團體之間的互動，澄清觀念，增加認知的改變，抒解壓力，學習如何去預防再犯，這都是我們的預防再犯的計畫。
2. 內容考慮犯罪方法、心態及次數	A：考慮到犯罪的手法、次數，他到底是用怎樣的一個心態再犯案？他在犯案之前到底是在想什麼？他是不是一個累犯？
	C：再犯的可能性，有些人故意把案情合理化、最小化，把案情講輕一點，我們從身分簿的記載和他的敘述來瞭解是否差異性很大。
評估受治療者成效	
1. 團體目標與表現	A：我強調團體的目標，另一方面我們也要參考他在團體的表現，是否真的有心要去轉變？
	B：看他參與團體治療後是否有悔悟，有沒有同理被害人的感受，他的情緒控制如何？
	C：自己可以同理被害人，計畫再犯預防的方法。
2. 自我覺察的能力	A：他對自己的問題瞭解的程度，我們是強調覺察的能力。他到底有沒有覺察到自己的狀態。
	C：他自己會認錯，願意去負責任。
	E：否認犯罪程度。
影響治療效能的因素	
1. 團體安全性	A：我覺得影響團體的成敗是這個團體是不是夠安全？同學是否願意分享私密？有些同學因為是害怕把自己的事蹟講出來後，會傳出去，造成自己的傷害而隱藏不說！
2. 團體時間與人數	A：因為團體治療時間16週，團體成員14人，時間短、人數略嫌多了些，會讓我們對每個人瞭解的程度，打

	一個折扣！
3.受治療者的動機	A：強制治療的字眼，感覺上好像缺乏動機，可是裡面還是有動機的，那這個強制治療就變有他的意義存在了。據我的觀察，大概只有一兩位還是有抗拒的心，或是動機性還是蠻薄弱的。大部分的團員透過這樣一次一次的團體治療，都會越來越投入。
	B：參與的動機很重要，主動性跟被動性就差很多了。主動性高就會很順利。
	D：我覺得亂倫組的防衛心強、抗拒，反反覆覆，有的時候承認，有的時候說是司法判處不公。
	E：治療過程中受治療者的治療動機，如果一直很虛偽的否認，只強調表面而不做深層的互動，會影響治療的效果。
4.治療者特質與技巧	A：治療師是不是夠受信賴，自己有沒有原則，有沒有覺得真的能夠幫助他們處理一些問題。
5.教材難易度	A：有些成員教育水準比較低，在唸課文的時候，他會有些意思不太能夠瞭解。教材還需要做一些修正，比如文化上的差異等。
	C：翻譯國外進來的東西，可能有本土文化適應上的問題，但是我們實在找不到更好的教材。
6.治療的場地與設施	A：場地有一張桌子當作遮蔽物，所以他身體很多非語言的動作，沒辦法觀察的那麼仔細！比如有些人可能很緊張，甚至會出現一些顫抖的現象或是肢體上訊息。
	C：有時候場地會換來換去。
7.治療時間	A：就預防再犯來看，因為團體人數比較多，16 週的時間要上課又要能夠談到每個人的問題，時間是相當的不足。
	D：治療時間 16 次蠻短的，國外治療時間都是一兩年，而且不斷地再教育，我們這邊性侵害的人太多，但治療的人太少。
	B：三個月治療時間，我個人覺得是不夠的。
治療的困境	
1.人力不足	C：最大的困難就是需要治療的人很多，監方一直說人力不足，我們盡力配合，但多少影響我們醫院的人力。
	E：治療人力是我最感困擾的，其實應該是由醫療相關人員進來。但是以我們目前十幾個治療師，大概只夠解決五分之一的案子。
2.擔憂人身安全	B：你不讓他通過，他可能出去之後會找你麻煩，我覺得

	安全需要顧慮。上課期間，他也會試探你在哪家個醫院上班？
	D：我們同事私底下會擔心，如果不讓他們通過，不知道他們出來以後，會找我怎麼樣？女孩子比較會擔心，畢竟他總是會出來嘛。
3.治療機構主體混淆不清	E：從制度面來講，本來監獄就不是執行醫療行為很適當的場所，應該放在醫院治療比較恰當，現在變成反客為主。目前全國監獄合格的醫師只有一位將近八十歲的老醫師，根本沒有治療的人力。
4.治療經費偏低	A：我覺得監獄有一點不公平的是醫師比其他人的待遇是高一倍，監獄裡面要作心理治療的話，我們所受的訓練絕對比醫生多，這是一個制度的問題！
	E：醫師的價碼比較高，做一樣的事，領不一樣的錢是很不公平的。
5.治療場所缺乏	B：強制治療的量多，而團體的地點有限，實在沒有足夠的空間。
6.專業訓練不足	B：我們也是第一次接觸性侵害的個案，所以經驗上比較不足，可能需要經驗的累積！

4.影響治療效能的因素：影響治療效能的因素諸多不一，根據治療者表示，受治療者對團體成員的信賴與主觀自覺的安全性、團體人數、參與團體的動機、治療者特質、教材難易度、治療場地以及治療時間等結構變數，都會影響治療的效益。團體成員之間是否信賴其實對於團體心理治療的進行有絕對性的影響，加上團體成員多，療程短，也就是說，團體的效果可能還沒有開始產生作用療程已經結束。如果其他的硬體與軟體設備無法配合，例如，教材太難、治療場地不固定、治療者無法安排適當的場地設置，治療效能受到諸多因數的混淆，必然無法適當的展現效果。

5.治療的困境：由面談看來，目前性侵害犯強制診療面臨的困難相當多仍待克服，主要有下列多項：人力不足、擔憂人身安全、治療機構主體混淆不清、治療經費偏低、治療場所缺乏、專業訓練不足等問題。關於治療者的部分，除了專業人員不足，專業上的在職訓練也相當缺乏，立法者訂定強制治療法案時並沒有適時的提出配套措施，導致對性侵害犯進行團體治療的美意付之闕如，也導致目前僅有的少數專業治療師對機構失去信心。

四、結論與建議

本研究以面對面訪談法，評估性侵害犯強制診療實施狀況，就受治療者與治療者之主客觀，探討強制診療方案執行情形與困境。

一、受治療者對強制治療之看法

1.受治療者有意願改變的動機是決定治療成功的最大因素，根據受治療者表示，多數參與治療的動機為提早假釋出獄，因此受治療者忽視了治療的本質，亦影響治療的成效。

2.除了部分受治療者抱著有心改過，而願意探索自己的問題。有些人則顧慮監獄特殊環境，時有防衛心理及抗拒行為出現。如自認無病不需治療；只談些無助治療的話題；不願為自己的行為負責；將自己所犯的錯誤怪罪於他人；與治療者玩時間遊戲，應付了事等。

3.多數參與治療者肯定團體治療，透過成員經驗的分享，可吸取他人優缺點，並增進自我覺察與反省能力，學習到解決問題的能力。

4.受治療者最擔心被貼標籤，被場舍的同學以歧視眼光看待，或在背後閒言閒語。嚴重的話，場舍的同學以找麻煩的方式羞辱，時有違規事件發生。

5.在治療前，受治療者的心情沉重、抑鬱，有罪惡感，無法釋懷。經由治療師教導後，成員漸漸瞭解過去的錯誤行為，抒解情感，凡事會考慮到對方的感受及後果。

「強制診療」一詞，雖然意味著性侵害犯被強迫接受治療，而性侵害犯對於何謂治療懵懵懂懂。團體治療初期，受治療者的動機不明顯，時有抗拒心理，隨著團體治療次數增加與治療師引導，由上述成員反映得知，受治療者漸漸理解與肯定團體治療效果，亦符合 Yalom（1995）「提供訊息」、「灌輸希望」、「宣洩」、「利他主義」、「模仿行為」等團體療效因素。

二、治療與行政人員對強制治療之看法

1.受治療者最擔憂治療評估是否通過而能提報假釋，治療成效評估之標準為何？受治療者常感疑慮與不解。受訪者評估治療成效的標準係依據受治療者的犯罪方法、心態與次數，在團體的表現與家庭作業及自我覺察等方面進行評定。

2.影響治療效能的因素諸多，受治療者的動機、團體安全性、團體人數、治療者特質、教材難易度、治療場地以及治療時間等團體結構，都會影響治療的效益。

3.目前性侵害犯強制診療面臨的困難有：人力不足、擔憂人身安全、治療機構主體混淆不清、治療經費偏低、治療場所缺乏、專業訓練不足等問題。

三、建議

1.治療前篩選成員並與溝通：本研究中發現，團體中有少數一、二位，抗拒治療，影響團體氣氛。治療人員對於團體成員，可事先晤談成員受治療意願，增進彼此了解，篩選適合參與團體治療的成員，以減少成員在團體中的抗拒行為，影響團體進行。

2.提高性侵害犯治療的意願：受治療者往往缺乏改變動機，其基本背景資料，多數已符合假釋條件，受治療者可能為爭取假釋，產生迎合治療者所好的虛偽表現。治療者須適度的提出面質，並提高個案參與感。

3.增加治療時間：再犯預防治療團體，治療期間為三個月，與美國密西根監獄為期一年半團體心理治療之比較，國內監獄治療期間稍嫌不足，影響評估成效，宜增加治療時間為六個月。

4.依課程內容設計評量工具：強制治療課程內容未經評估，且主題施教未有評量工具，無法得知成員學習效果，宜根據課程內容，設計評量工具。

5.聘請專家學者編寫教材：有關治療性侵害犯教材不多見，目前以使用Freeman-Longo et al. (1995)之「我是誰，我為何要接受治療？」、「我為何再犯？」及「我如何阻止再犯？」等三本翻譯教材為主，其內容不盡符合國情，應積極聘請專家學者編寫教材。

6.刑中與刑前之受治療者應分開治療：團體成員有刑中之受刑人與刑前之受處分人混合治療，惟其有不同刑行處遇與法律效果，彼此期待迥異，影響治療效果。

7.不同類型的性侵害犯需不同治療計劃：不同類型的性侵害犯，有不同犯罪成因與特質。目前監獄對於性侵害犯治療，約略分為強姦犯、亂倫兩組，以再犯預防之認知行為療法為取向，但對於性暴力連續犯是否適用，不無疑問。因此，根據性侵害犯不同犯罪手法、人格特質、早年生活經驗，細分性侵害犯類型，輔以其他理論技術（如依附理論），訂定不同治療處遇計畫。

　　8.治療評估成效之標準化：受治療者相當重視是否通過治療評估，並有不同程度期待與疑慮，影響治療者與被治療者之專業關係。應建立標準化治療評估基準，以昭公信。

　　9.建構完善醫療網：目前性侵害犯的強制診療體系，分為刑前鑑定，獄中治療，出獄後社區身心治療。其中監獄負責治療業務，由於尋求治療人員不易，壓力相當沉重，然而專責治療的衛生署，無法統籌支援治療人力，任由監獄四處求援碰壁，影響治療時程。衛生署首當整合醫療體系，協助監獄支援治療人力，使監獄無後顧之憂。

　　10.善用民間資源：治療人員長期的不足乃影響推動強制治療最大的問題，除了繼續尋求公立醫療機構支援外，可納入民營有證照之心理師或社工師的介入，如00工作坊或治療室，以提高專業人員參與。

　　11.追蹤受治療者再犯率：為了解性侵害犯接受監獄治療之再犯率，宜委託學術機構，從事研究受治療者出獄後之再犯率，以檢視治療計劃是否有效性，並藉以修訂治療計畫內容。

五、參考文獻

(一)中文部分

李思賢、趙育慧、黃沛銓、吳慶蘭、呂瑩純（2002）：〈台灣地區醫學生性知識來源、性態度與性行為調查〉。《台灣性學學刊》，8卷2期，頁15-27。

周煌智、陳筱萍、郭壽宏、張永源（2000）：〈性侵害加害人的特徵與治療策略〉。《公共衛生》，27卷1期，頁1-13。

侯崇文、周愫嫻、吳建昌、林惠華、胡佳吟（2000）：《性侵害案件偵查心理描繪技術運用》。台北：內政部性侵害防治委員會。

許春金、馬傳鎮（1999）：《台灣地區性侵害犯罪狀況與型態之調查研究》。桃園：中央警察大學犯罪防治研究所。

陳若璋（2001）：《性罪犯心理學心理治療與評估》。台北：張老師文化圖書公司。

黃軍義（2000）：〈強姦犯罪的心理歷程：（一）理論分析〉。《本土心理學研究》，13期，頁3-52。

黃軍義、陳若璋（1997）：《強姦犯罪成因及相關之研究》。台北：法務部。

黃富源（1995）：〈情色傳媒與性暴力研究之文獻探討〉。《警學叢刊》，2卷25期，頁101-118。

黃富源、黃徵男、范瓊方、廖有祿、周文勇、許福生、黃翠紋、廖訓誠、藍慶煌、黃家珍（1999）：《性侵害加害人之特質與犯罪手法之研究》。台北：內政部性侵害防治委員會。

羅燦瑛（1994）：《熟識強暴的媒體建構—中國時報對「師大案」及「胡李案」新聞報導之本文分析與比較》。台北：女性與新聞傳播研討會。

(二)外文部分

Baron, L. & Straus, M.（1987）Four theories of rape: a macro-sociological analysis. *Social Problems*, 34, 467-489.

Baron, L. & Straus, M.（1989）*Four theories of rape in American society: A state-level analysis*. New Haven: Yale University Press.

Blau, J. R. & Blau, P.（1982）The cost inequality: metropolitan structure and violent crime. *American Sociological Review*, 47, 114-128.

Blau, P., & Golden, R.（1986）Metropolitan structure and criminal violence. *Sociological Quarterly*, 27, 15-26.

Freeman-Longo, R., Bird, S., Stevenson, W. F., & Fiske, J. A.（1995）1994 *Nationwide survey of treatment programs and models: Serving abuse reaction children and adolescent and adult sex offenders*. VT: Safer Society Program & Press.

Marshall, L.（1988）The use of sexually explicit stimuli by rapist, child molesters, and non-offenders. *Journal of Sex Research*, 25, 267-288.

Smith, M. & Bennett, N.（1987）Poverty, inequality, and theories of forcible rape. *Crime and Delinquency*, 31, 295-305.

Wolf, S.C.（1984）*A Multifactor Model of Deviant Sexuality*. Paper Present at the Third International Conference on Victimology, Lisbon.

Yalom, I. D.（1995）*The theory and practice of group psychotherapy*. (4th Ed.). New York: A Member of Perseus Books Group.

附錄一、性侵害犯強制診療訪談大綱

　　本研究爲瞭解治療人員及性侵害犯，對性侵害強制治療之評價與實施困境之看法，請依個人知悉的狀況對下列各題目，提供寶貴意見，以作未來強制治療改進之參考。

㈠治療人員部分

　　1.您對性侵害犯治療，採取何種治療模式與內容？

　　2.您如何評估性侵害犯治療效能？

　　3.您認爲影響性侵害犯治療效能因素爲何？（基本背景與動機、教材或書籍、受刑人監獄次文化、監獄行政組織）

　　4.您認爲治療性侵害犯困境爲何？（專業治療人員數量、人員專業知能與訓練、治療場所改進之處、教育課程或自助團體、設備或儀器、業務經費、治療時間、社會資源、法務部與衛生署溝通協調與權責劃分等）

㈡性侵害犯部分

　　1.您對於被強制治療的看法，接受治療動機爲何？

　　2.您是否意願接受治療，治療過程的感受爲何？

　　＊您參與團療態度爲何？

　　＊您覺得團療對您有何助益？

　　＊您同房同學對您接受治療有何看法？

　　＊您對所接受的治療人員、態度、技術，感覺爲何？

　　＊您認爲在治療前與治療後有何差別？

　　3.您對治療課程有何建議？

從庾信〈傷王司徒褒〉一詩探討庾信與王褒之交誼

葉慕蘭

國防醫學院

人文及社會科學科副教授

摘　　要

　　庾信、王褒倆人本出生在南朝梁武帝太平時代，王褒出身具有盛名的高門；庾信在梁代是著名的宮體詩人，倆人分別是梁簡文帝蕭綱、梁元帝蕭繹文學集團的文士。梁武帝晚年，因為侯景之亂，此亂遍及江東全境，餘波禍及江陵，未幾即有江陵之亡，倆人相繼被迫離開南朝梁而成為梁末羈北的文士，從此不得南返。由於倆人有文才與學養，而成為由南入北的北朝文壇領袖。本文試從庾信〈傷王司徒褒〉一詩來探析庾信與王褒之交誼。

關鍵字：庾信、王褒、侯景、古詩

壹、前言

　　庾信、王褒都生活在動蕩的南北朝後期，兩人本出生在南朝梁武帝時代，武帝在位有四十八年之久，改過七次年號。他即位之初的天監十七年中，文治武功並盛，史稱「天監之治」。可惜好景不長，他晚年倦於政事而迷信佛教，弄得朝綱不振，法紀蕩然。就在這時突然發生了一幕掀天動地的侯景之亂，打破了南北平衡對峙之局，弄得梁朝分崩離析而亡 1。庾信、王褒都因為侯景之亂、江陵之亡而相繼被迫離開南朝梁，而成為梁末羈北文士。庾信、王褒入北之後對北朝的政治文化發生影響，兩人同時成為北朝文壇領袖，他們的詩賦駢文不但在南北文化的交流方面立下功勳，而且在南北時期的文學向唐朝文學的轉折過程中，有者劃時代的意義。庾信、王褒可謂同是天涯淪落人，為此王褒一旦謝世，庾信有「閒坐悲君亦自悲，百年都是幾多時？」（唐、元稹〈遣悲懷之三〉）千古浩歎，更有潘岳〈悼亡詩〉：「賦詩欲言志，此志難具紀。命也可奈何，長戚自令鄙。」長期陷入痛苦之中「命也可奈何」的沈鬱頓挫之無奈。此情此意可從庾信〈傷王司徒褒〉一詩中感受到。

　　庾信〈西元五一三─五八一年〉字子山，小字蘭成，祖籍南陽新野人（今河南省新野縣）。父親庾肩吾是梁代著名的宮體詩人。庾家父子和徐摛，徐陵父子一起出入宮廷，寫作綺麗的詩文，著名於當時，號稱「徐庾體」[2]。梁武帝太清年間侯景之亂，他領兵作戰，兵敗後逃避江陵，在梁元帝蕭繹手下做官，元帝承聖三年（西元五五五年）奉帝之命出使西魏。到長安不久，西魏攻打江陵，元帝被俘遇害，梁亡。他從此羈留北方，歷事西魏、北周，直到隋文帝開皇元年（西元五八一年）過世。他的作品以他四十二歲出使西魏為分界限，分為前後兩期，前期作品乃是在南朝梁時的作品，此時作品先後在侯景之亂、江陵之亡中散佚。他後期作品乃是指入北以後的作品，這些作品在他六十七歲時，由北周滕王宇文逌為他編成《庾信集》二十卷兩帙本，並為此集作序予以宣揚，才得以傳播於世。至於庾信的作品，今存的集子是宋人編的，清・倪璠〈庾子山集題辭〉曰：

　　世之所謂《庾開府集》，本宋太宗諸臣所輯，分類鳩聚後人抄撰成書，故其中多不詮次，取而注之，文集凡十有六卷 [3]

　　《庾集》之注本隋時已有，《隋書、魏澹傳》云：「太子勇令注庾集世稱其博物」[4]。到了清代《庾集》出現兩家注本，一是吳兆宜的《庾開府集箋注》十卷，一是倪璠的，《庾子山集》十六卷，吳本較疏略，倪本考核史實，旁採博搜較吳本詳實。故倪本十六卷為研究庾信作品之通行本。本文以倪注本為主。

貳、從庾信〈傷王司徒褒〉一詩探討庾信與王褒之交誼

一、庾信〈傷王司徒褒〉一詩析論

　　庾信、王褒北遷後成爲羈旅之臣，故王褒之死對庾信產生了另一種強烈的打擊。根據推測，王褒大約死於北周武帝建德五年（西元五七六年）左右，他死在宜州刺史任內，享年六十四歲。和庾信的年齡大致相同，從詩中可見庾信的悲痛。

　　昔聞王子晉，輕舉逐神仙
　　謂言君積善，還得嗣前賢。
　　四海皆流寓，非爲獨播遷。
　　豈意中台坼，君當風燭前。
　　自君鐘鼎族，江東三百年。
　　寶刀仍世載，琱戈本舊傳。
　　綠綬紆槐綬，黃金飾侍蟬。
　　地建忠臣國，家開孝子泉。
　　自能枯木潤，足得流水圓。
　　以君承祖武，諸侯無間然。
　　青衿已對日，童子即論天。
　　穎陰珠玉麗，河陽脂粉妍。
　　名高六國共，價重十城連。
　　辯足觀秋水，文堪題馬鞭。
　　迴鸞抱書字，別鶴繞琴弦。
　　擁旄裁甸服，垂帷非被邊。
　　靜亭空繫馬，閑烽直起煙。
　　不廢披書案，無妨坐釣船。
　　茂陵忽多病，淮陽實未痊。
　　侍醫逾默默，神理遂綿綿。
　　永別張平子，長埋王仲宣。
　　柏谷移松樹，陽陵買墓田。
　　陝路秋風起，寒堂已颯颯。
　　邱楊一搖落，山火即時然。
　　昔爲人所羨，今爲人所憐。
　　世途旦復旦，人情玄又玄，

故人傷此別，留恨滿秦川。

定名於此定，全德以斯全。

惟有山陽笛，悽余思舊篇。〈傷王司徒褒〉

詩題為〈傷王司徒褒〉把王褒的官名寫作「司徒」，這是地方官府的長官，但王褒沒有作過這樣的官位，王褒在擔任宜州刺史的官職是小司空，也就是多官府的次長，「司空」誤抄成「司徒」，詩題宜為「傷王司空褒」。王褒逝世時，庾信正擔任洛州刺史，住在洛陽，當他接到友人訃聞，感傷的寫下這首哀悼詩5。全詩為五言古詩，共有五十八句，押平聲韻—「仙、先」通韻，平仄的安排五十八句中合律句者共有四十二句。全詩的內容可分三大部分：

第一部分，從第一句至第八句為總寫：

昔聞王子晉，輕舉逐神仙。

謂言君積善，還得嗣前賢。

四海皆流寓，非為獨播遷。

豈意中台坼，君當風燭前。

這八句意謂：「聽說古代的王子晉，當了神仙後乘升天。你生前廣積善行，大家都說你會繼承前代賢者之後。人生如寄四海之內，皆為流寓之所，何必離家才算播遷呢？意想不到的是，中台星裂開，你的生命竟變成風前的燭光。」6 追述王褒先人，及其本人之成就，無奈他身逢亂世，羈旅北方，而今又在風燭中隨風而逝。用語自然平淺流圓，但含意豐富，傷感之情潺潺而出，淡淡之交，曖曖含光。

第二部分，從第九句至第三十六句分敘王褒之生平事蹟，又可分兩部分述之：

㈠從第九句至第十八句：

自君鐘鼎族，將東三百年。

寶刀仍世載，琱戈本舊傳。

綠綬紆槐綬，黃金飾侍蟬。

地建忠臣國，家開孝子泉。

自能枯木潤，足得流水圓。

這十句意謂：「王君出身在富貴名門，家在南朝，繁榮達三百年。祖先的寶刀代代相承，以玉做裝飾的戈象徵先人的偉業。有的人擔任宰相，佩戴綠色的印綬；有的則擔任侍中，戴上用蟬羽裝飾的金冠。受到頒賜領地建國，世代又如泉水般不斷湧現孝子。由於有漂亮的玉，使枯木都得到滋潤；只要有好存在，就連水流都會為之改變。」[7]，敘述王氏在東晉、宋、南齊、梁四個朝代的豐功偉業，均任宰相、侍中等職。更是道德高尚，其中以孝為傳家之寶，為此代代出傑出人物，影響後代。王褒身受先人庇蔭。：

　　(二)從第十九句至第三十六句：

　　　　以君承祖武，諸侯無間然。

　　　　青衿已對日，童子即論天。

　　　　穎陰珠玉麗，河陽脂粉妍。

　　　　名高六國共，價重十城連。

　　　　辯足觀秋水，文堪題馬鞭。

　　　　迴鸞抱書子，別鶴繞琴弦。

　　　　擁旄裁旬服，垂帷非被邊。

　　　　靜亭空繫馬，閑烽直起煙。

　　　　不廢披書案，無妨坐釣船。

　　這十八句意謂：「你繼承父祖之後，就任諸侯爵位，也沒有任何人感到不滿，都認為實至名歸。在求學時期，就能回答關於日蝕的問題，自幼小就喜歡談論天文。就像穎陰有珠玉般美麗的女人，河陽的宅邸有美豔的脂粉一般，你的婚姻十分美滿。名望之高，使人想到六國宰相蘇秦；價值之重，足以和需要十五城池交換的璧玉匹敵。滔滔辯才，如秋水般流暢；文思泉湧，能在馬鞭上立刻成章。書法之妙，有如飛舞的鸞鳥，和文字融成一體。奏琴之精，連孤獨的鶴心也被吸引。司令官的力量所及之處，是只有離開王城二十里的範圍。在邊境你的才能已經無法發揮。驛亭靜悄悄的，馬仍栓在那兒，沒想到通報緊急情況的烽火卻突然升了起來結果你不能成為離開辦公桌的武將，只有走上在釣魚時才被周文王發現的呂尚輔佐命運。」[8] 先從王褒仕途敘起「起家祕書郎，轉太子舍人，襲爵南昌縣侯」（《周書、王褒傳》），又敘述王褒之早慧和才華，由於有才華而受到梁武帝的喜愛，於是「梁武帝喜其才藝，遂以弟鄱陽王恢之女妻之」（《周書、王褒傳》），運用「穎陰珠玉麗，河陽脂粉妍」典故，就是指王褒的婚姻。接下者運用的典故，再說明王褒的辯才、書藝等才藝。無奈侯景之亂，梁朝國勢衰微，梁元帝蕭繹即位江陵，王褒因與元帝舊交，受委重任，拜吏部尚書右僕射。「靜亭空繫馬，閑烽直起煙。不廢披書案，無妨坐釣船。」這兩句說明西魏攻破江陵，王褒隨元帝出降，王褒像姜太公呂尚以漁釣周西伯，遇到北周宇文泰的賞識。

　　第二部分從王褒的少年時期開始描述，直到梁朝亡國後到北方的過程。

　　第三部分，從第三十七句至第五十八句：

　　　　茂陵忽多病，淮陽實未瘳。

　　　　侍醫逾默默，神理遂綿綿。

　　　　永別張平子，長埋王仲宣。

　　　　柏谷移松樹，陽陵買墓田。

　　　　陝路秋風起，寒堂已颯焉。

　　　　邱楊一搖落，山火即時然。

　　　　昔爲人所羨，今爲人所憐。

　　　　世途旦復旦，人情玄又玄。

　　　　故人傷此別，留恨滿秦川。

　　　　定名於此定，全德以斯全。

　　　　惟有山陽笛，悽余思舊篇。

　　這二十二句意謂：「茂陵的詩人突然變得多病起來，在淮陽修養也不見很好的效果。侍醫看過病情以後，神態更加沉默了；而你的精神最後也離開軀體，將要永存在這世上。和才可比做張衡的你永別，你從此就步隨者當年才子王粲，走上黃泉之路了。過去的你，是個令人羨慕的對象，如今卻變成讓人憐憫的靈魂；人世日復一日的轉移，世人對你的懷念也會逐漸模糊。我是你的老友，對這次被永別非常傷心，遺憾的念頭充塞整個秦川之地。如果人的名聲有定論，如今也是有個定論的時刻；如果人的品性能達全德，現在也該是達到的時候了。只是，一旦經過你曾住過的地方，聽到陣陣笛聲，在我回顧彼此友情的詩裡，便會憑添無限沉痛的思念。」9最後這二十二句中，可看出庾信對王褒之死產生出無限的感慨，尤其「世途旦復旦，人情玄又玄。故人傷此別，留恨滿秦川。定名於此定，全德以斯全。」對人間世充滿無限感慨，無奈；悲傷王褒的死亡，或許其他人逐漸忘了，而命運與王褒相近的庾信卻是「留恨滿秦川」沉痛孤寂，令人心酸。庾信、王褒兩人年過四十後,相繼遭侯景之亂，江陵之禍，彼此有同病相憐的共鳴，庾信很在乎：「定名於此定，全德以斯德」，借王褒之死為王褒「定名」、「全德」，也為自己下定論。由於庾信自小受儒家教育，父子又受梁朝恩典，不得已羈北，因此他很在乎別人的看法，歷史對他的評價，為此他後期作品中往往流露出羈北出仕之矛盾與羞愧感。總之，這首長詩的內容，一面回顧王褒的一生，一面對王褒之死寄予感慨，造語平淡，運典自然，於平淡寄予沉痛壓抑的感情，一死一生乃知交情，因此從此詩來探討兩人之交誼。

二、從庾信〈傷王司徒褒〉一詩探討庾信與王褒之交誼

從庾信〈傷王司徒褒〉一詩中「昔為人所羨，今為人所憐。世途旦復旦，人情玄又玄。故人傷此別，留恨滿秦川。定名於此定，全德以斯全。惟有山陽笛，悽余思舊篇。」，庾信深知入北後屈仕北朝之心情，「定名於此定，全德以斯全。惟有山陽笛，悽余思舊篇。」庾信運用晉、向秀〈思舊賦〉思念逝世友人嵇康、呂安而追思與王褒之情。「閒坐悲君亦自悲」（唐、元稹〈遣悲懷之三〉）總評王褒一生，也評論了自己。本文試從㈠仕宦梁朝㈡中年際遇㈢唱和之作三方面一探庾信與王褒之交誼：

㈠仕宦梁朝

王褒〈西元五一四—五五七年〉10 字子淵，祖籍瑯琊臨沂人〈今山東臨沂〉。「識量淵通，志懷沉靜，美風儀，善談笑，博覽史傳，尤工屬文」11。出身江南望族—瑯琊王氏；自西漢武帝時，王吉為開創瑯琊王氏一族經學家傳之祖。經三百餘年入魏晉間，王氏經學首推王祥。東晉南朝，崇尚文章，儒風不整。南齊儒學卻大盛，乃是當時名臣王儉之力 12，王儉是王褒曾祖父，王儉是南齊政治界和文學界實力人物，他詳悉故實深為當道者所倚重，亦成為保持祿位之一重要倚憑。王褒祖父王騫缺乏文才和聲望，因父之庇蔭而在朝為官。父王規，為梁侍中。故齊、梁二代，王氏在政壇上的勢力依然。在姻戚方面：聯姻宗室，廣結權貴，如王褒姑母嫁予梁簡文帝蕭綱為妃，梁國子祭酒蕭子雲是王褒的姑夫。梁武帝愛其才，以弟鄱陽王蕭灰之女妻之。在文化方面：王褒曾祖父王儉在南齊時代大振儒學隱然為當時議禮名家之首，他曾校訂典籍獻〈七志〉，〈元徽四部〉，上表文甚為雅典 13。王

褒博覽史傳，尤工屬文外，他在草隸書法方面有傑出才能，《周書、王褒傳》：「梁國子祭酒蕭子雲，褒之姑夫也，特善草隸，褒少以姻戚，去來其家，遂相模範。俄而名亞子雲，並重於世。」14 於此可知王褒對書法之喜愛，一者受蕭子雲影響，一者是天賦所使然。王褒在書法上有很大成就。在仕途方面：王褒的仕宦，《周書、王褒傳》：「起家秘書郎，轉太子舍人」這是一條甲族既定的仕宦道路，以後他「襲爵南昌縣侯，稍遷祕書丞，于時盛選僚佐，乃以褒為文學，尋遷安成郡守。」15，世族的政治地位，可賴其父祖餘蔭。於此可知王褒年輕時在梁之政治，社會地位之優越。

總之，瑯琊王氏的王褒在梁朝受到尊敬和禮遇，故明、張溥〈後周王司空集題詞〉評曰：「瑯琊世胄，文學名位，照耀江左，子淵又以蕭祭酒姻戚，聲華萼跗，遂至王女下降，國嫡用賓」16。王褒在侯景之亂之前，過者士族冠冕，累世簪纓，享受祿位的生活。

庾信生平前文已述，他仕宦道路，據《周書、庾信傳》所述：「起家湘東國常侍，轉安南府參軍。遷尚書度支郎中，通直正員郎。」17 庾氏自漢末庾乘以來，迄於晉代，人位盛顯，冠冕當世。庾峻與王祥、王覽等同朝。渡江之後，庾亮、庾翼、庾冰各據要津，使諸王側目 18。而在此時，庾氏本居潁川鄢陵。至此有部分已徙居南陽新野。庾信八世祖滔即已遷居新野一地 19。庾信之八世祖滔又隨晉元帝渡江，遷至江陵宋玉之舊宅，因此庾氏先祖，可說是北方士族血統之後裔，這種出身，使得庾信之家族受到貴門世族之教養。於此可知重視門閥世族時期，世家大族競以姓望邑里相矜，論門閥庾信出身比不上王褒。

南朝寒門世族起家的皇帝為穩定社會需要高門世族的支持，皇帝一方面禮遇他們，另一方面提倡詩文創作。齊、梁時代每個帝王都不僅重視文學，而且身兼作者，這樣就形成了以帝王為中心的文學集團，而這些世家子弟作者，又多依附于當時的帝王。庾信，王褒分別是梁簡文帝蕭綱，梁元帝蕭繹文學集團的文士 20，蕭綱、蕭繹兄弟的文學主張是新變派，代表人物為庾肩吾、庾信父子以及徐摛、徐陵父子。蕭綱是宮體詩的首創者，蕭繹附之 21。庾信十九歲便成為宮體詩高手，由于徐、庾父子文名重于一時，世人稱其文章為"徐庾體 22"。由於東晉南朝，崇尚文章，儒風不振，經學不興，齊梁文壇："宮體所傳，且變朝野 23"。此種盛況下，庾信文名遠播：「當時後進競相模範，每有一文，京都莫不傳頌。」（《周書、庾信傳》）。有梁時代庾信文名大於重視經學，書法，應用文字的王褒。

　　庾信、王褒出生在梁武帝太平時代。王褒出身具有盛名的高門，個人「識量淵通，志懷沉靜，美風儀，善談笑」（《周書、王褒傳》），為人愼獨謙遜，具有經綸之才，又是皇室的外戚，所以得到繼承武帝政權的皇太子蕭綱─簡文帝和皇太孫蕭大心的信任和禮遇，過得是青雲直上的年輕甲族生活。庾信並非為甲族子弟，由於君王愛好文學，文學之士的地位也隨之高升，他屬於簡文帝文學集團中一名宮體詩詩人，他的文名都在其他文學侍臣之上24。無奈侯景之亂，江陵之亡改變兩人的命運，也促成兩人之相知。

　　㈡中年際遇

　　梁武帝太清二年（西元五四八年）侯景的軍隊渡江南下，直攻建康城。侯景亂起，建康殘破，此時湘東王蕭繹為荊州刺史鎮江陵，他命陳霸先、王僧辯攻打侯景，終於在承聖元年〈西元五五二年〉四月，平定這個前後三年零八月的大亂，從此梁室分裂，士族流離失所，士族僥倖得保性命的，多數西逃荊州，往依梁元帝蕭繹。庾信、王褒便是在這種狀況下來到江陵，此時庾信、王褒正值三十九、四十歲。現分1、在江陵時的庾信與王褒，2、羈留北朝的庾信與王褒，兩方面敘述之：

　　1.在江陵時的庾信與王褒

　　庾信在梁武帝大同十一年（西元五四五年）出使東魏成績卓著，返國後，三十四歲調升到京城建康為「東宮學士，領建康令」25，不幸，梁武帝太清二年（西元五四八年）侯景攻陷建康，庾信是建康令，守朱雀航，他「見景皆著鐵面，退隱于門。信方食甘蔗，有飛箭中門柱，信手甘蔗，應弦而落，遂棄軍走。」26 庾信不戰而退。翌年，侯景陷台城庾信開始投奔江陵。他到了江陵先任御史中丞，承聖元年（西元五五一年）轉右衛將軍封武康縣。此時梁室分崩離析，承聖二年（西元五五二年）武陵王蕭紀將兵東下進攻江陵，梁元帝蕭繹在承聖三年（西元五五四年）四月派庾信求救於西魏，九月西魏軍就攻陷了江陵。庾信成為人質被扣留在長安，時年四十二歲，從此以後他再也不能回到南朝國土。

　　梁武帝太清二年（西元五四八年）侯景的軍隊攻下建康時，王褒任安成內史時表現非凡，《周書、王褒傳》：「宣成王大器，簡文帝之冢嫡，即褒之姑子也。于時盛選僚佐，乃以褒為文學，尋遷安成郡守。及侯景渡江，建業擾亂，褒輯寧所部，見稱於時」27。梁元帝在承聖元年（西元五五二年），王僧辯平定了侯景之亂後，同年十一月，梁元帝蕭繹即位於江陵。王褒與梁元帝有很深的關係，深受元帝賞識，元帝登位，王褒因舊交之情受委重任，拜侍中，吏部尚書，左僕射28。王褒高門世族，他具有「旣世冑名家，文學優贍，當時咸相推揖」29的崇高聲望來懷柔建康的貴族，元帝以王褒來穩定江陵政權。元帝是個「稟性猜忌，不隔疏近，御下無術」的皇帝30，王褒雖「旬月之間，位升端右，寵遇日隆，而褒愈自謙虛，不以位地矜人，時論稱之」31。王褒貌似受重用，但在重要的問題上元帝根本不採納王褒的意見：當時一些出生在江陵的人主張定都江陵，另一些來自長江下游的人則主張還都建康。大家在朝討論時，王褒也在場，元帝「顧謂褒等曰：“卿意以為何如？”褒性謹慎，知元帝猜忌，弗敢公言其非，當時唯唯而已。」32。王褒曾趁間密諫，力主還建康，但元帝未加採納。總之，王褒在元帝朝平安無事地做了三年（承聖元年—承聖三年）的高官。

王褒與庾信本為簡文帝蕭綱文學集團文士，侯景之亂之後，西依荊州江陵蕭繹時，再度成為蕭繹文學集團文士。這文學集團的文學活動中有關庾信與王褒有唱和之作的，據《周書、王褒傳》：「褒曾作〈燕歌行〉，妙盡關塞寒苦之狀，元帝及諸文士並和之，而競為淒切之詞。」33諸文士包括庾信在內，今王褒，蕭繹，庾信之作乃存。於此可見庾信與王褒互動的紀錄。於此可見庾信與王褒交誼的自然。侯景之亂以後，庾信與王褒同時侍持梁元帝，但元帝不思遷都，

元帝猜忌兇狠，以至同室操戈，骨肉相殘，叔姪分別向北齊、西魏求援。元帝承聖二年（西元五五四年）四月庾信出使西魏，九月宇文泰派兵攻打江陵，元帝臨陣督軍，此時王褒受命都督城西諸軍事，王褒盡忠勤之節。被圍之後，上下猜忌，元帝唯於褒深相委信，王褒從元帝入子城，不久江陵失陷，元帝出降，王褒也被迫出見西魏將領于謹，幷隨之入長安。庾信與王褒從此成為梁末羈北文士，兩人命運相似，同病相憐，相知相惜，友誼自然不同於南朝。

2. 羈留北朝的庾信與王褒

王褒於梁元帝承聖三年（西元五五四年）十二月，與王克，劉瑴，殷不

害等數十人，被俘入長安，受到西魏丞相宇文太泰（北周文皇帝）的接見，宇文泰高興對這一行人說：「昔平吳之利，二陸而已。今定楚之功，群賢畢至。可謂過之矣。」，更對王褒和王克說：「吾即王氏甥也，卿等並吾之舅氏，當以親戚爲情，勿以去鄉介意。」[34] 魏末的動亂造就了宇文泰崛起的機會，他建立起一個以關中爲本位的政治集團，利用關中世族蘇綽等，根據周禮建立官制，欲建立強大的政治集團。以當時東魏，西魏及南方的梁這三個政權比較，不論是從人力或財富而論，西魏遠比東魏差，比起南梁也遜得多。從文化基礎來說，東魏承受北魏孝文帝漢以來的文明，梁則是中國正統文化所在地，這些都是當時荒殘僻陋的關隴地區難以比配的[35]。因此王褒等南方文人被俘到長安，可見宇文泰迎接之殷切。於是授「褒車騎大將軍，儀同三司。常從容上席，資餼甚厚。褒等亦並荷恩眄，忘其羈旅焉。」宇文泰以獲南方人才而樂。西魏恭帝三年（西元五五六年）宇文泰死後，第三子宇文覺受魏之禪讓創立周王朝，即北周孝閔帝。孝閔帝元年，王褒「封石泉縣子，邑三百戶。」同年九月，孝閔帝被殺，宇文毓明帝即位，「世宗即位，篤好文學。時褒與庾信才名最高，特加親待。帝每遊宴，命褒等賦詩談論，常在左右尋加開府儀同三司」，明帝是一個愛好文學的皇帝，他自己賦詩（有〈和王褒詠摘花〉），甚至集諸文士於麟趾殿進行校訂和編纂經史的工作。王褒爲麟趾學士[36]。明帝宇文毓遇害，遺詔宇文邕繼位，即北周武帝，武帝爲宇文泰第四子，與閔帝，明帝皆不同母。武帝爲一明敏有主見，有遠識，據有雄才大略的皇帝。由南入北的高門世族瑯琊王褒，在武帝「保定中除內史中大夫」內史是與皇帝較接近的官僚。保定二年（西元五六二年），南朝陳文帝以其弟瑱（宣帝）在北周，而欲與周和，派尙書周弘正往長安迎宣帝，周弘正在長安留三年之久，於保定二年（西元五六二年）周弘正才自周返國，周弘正爲王褒好友周弘讓之弟，與王褒等通音信。王褒侍在武帝身側，建德元年（西元五七二年）武帝殺了太師宇文護，開始親政，武帝便重用王褒長才「褒有器局，雅識治體，既累世在江東爲宰輔，高祖亦以此重之。建德以後，頗參朝議，凡大詔冊，皆令褒具草」。武帝重用王褒世家爲宰輔之行政經驗，爲周室草佈詔命，位極人臣。同年四月，魯國公宇文贇立太子後，王褒「東宮既建，授太子少保，遷小司空，仍掌綸誥。乘輿行幸，褒常侍從。尋出爲宜州刺史，卒于位。時年六十四。」王褒以其個人學養與其世家出身，在異國受到優厚的禮遇，官場上之得意，實不下於在南朝梁時。

庾信從梁元帝承聖三年（西元五五四年）四月，奉元帝之命出使西魏。當他到長安尚未完成使命時，西魏就於九月決定派宇瑾等人率兵會同蕭察進攻江陵，並在十月正式出兵，十二月，蕭繹被殺，庾信從此被留在北方，在長安他被扣留坐牢，〈哀江南賦序〉曰：「華陽奔命，有去無歸。中興道銷。窮於甲戌。三日哭於都亭，三年囚於別館」描述他被魏所執，囚於別館的傷痛。由於北朝君臣一向傾慕南方文學，庾信又久負盛名，宇文泰爲鞏固政權，爲利用庾信的文才，於是釋放庾信，而「拜使持節撫軍將軍，右金紫光祿大夫，大都督。尋進車騎大將軍儀同三司。」北周宇文覺在西元五五七年取代西魏恭帝地位，即爲孝閔帝，庾信除「封臨清縣子，邑五百戶。除司水下大夫」。明帝宇文毓時出爲「弘農郡守」。武帝宇文邕時爲「司憲中大夫，進爵義城縣侯，俄拜洛州刺史」，在洛州刺史頗有治績，《周書、庾信傳》：「拜洛州刺史，信多識舊章，爲政簡靜，吏民安之。」庾信以南方文士受到北周國君賞識，尤其明帝，武帝都愛好文學，庾信再度成爲文學侍從，武帝天和三年（西元五六八年）八月，北周、北齊言和，兩國互派使者通好，庾信奉命接待北齊使者，又出使北齊。總之，庾信出仕西魏，再仕北周，在北周蒙受明帝，武帝賞識。依然發揮他的文才，在北周文壇地位崇高，成爲王公貴族仰慕的對象。庾信被羈留北方，一直沒有南歸，屈仕西魏、北周，雖蒙恩禮，但在他心深處卻懷極大的矛盾與掙扎，爲此他後期作品充滿鄉關之思。

庾信與王褒因侯景之亂，江陵之禍，相繼入北。當宇文泰主政西魏時，爲求賢，對梁末羈北文學之士庾信囚於別館，先兵後禮。而對瑯琊王褒卻別以甥舅相稱，以收買高門士族，到武帝便用王褒之行政經驗，經國之大手筆，爲周室草擬詔命，因此王褒在北周位極人臣，忘其羈旅，過得是得天獨厚的生活。王褒以政治才略受到北周諸君王進用。而庾信以文學擅長，他在南朝梁便以"徐、庾體"聞名於世，入北朝周王室貴族都慕其名，尤其趙王宇文招特別向他學庾信體，創作了很多經豔的詩。又與滕王宇文逌的關係密切，以至於大象元年（西元五七九年）爲庾信編撰《庾信集》二十卷，並爲之作序，使庾信作品得以流傳。庾信與王褒在北周力求漢化，又一心定天下的經營下，因此這兩個梁末文士成了不可缺少的人才，故武帝建德四年〈西元五七五年〉，當時南朝陳要求王襃、庾信等十幾人回國，武帝不放庾信、王襃，《周書、、庾信傳》：「時陳氏與朝廷通好，南北流寓之士，各許還其舊國。高祖唯放王克、殷不害等，信及襃並留而不遣。」於此可見兩人的文才對北周的影響，如武帝保定元年〈西元五六一年〉即位，雖行周禮，未臻雅正，天和元年初造〈山雲舞〉，以備六代，至建德三年樂成，始有可觀。這六代樂的歌辭便是庾信創作，庾信巧妙地利用北周朝廷令其制作郊廟歌辭的機會，向當權者反復宣揚漢民族悠久的文化和儒家傳統的文藝觀，加快鮮卑族漢化近程 37。北周武帝是個雄才大略的國君，王襃是一個高門士族，有器局，雅識治體，又能參預朝議，草擬詔冊的宰相之才。庾信是具有文學才華的幕僚文士，在北周「群公碑誌，多相請託。唯王襃頗與信相埒，自餘文人莫有逮者。」於此可見庾信和王襃兩人身處異國，王襃參預朝議，政治地位極高，而庾信只是幕僚的文學侍從。他們在北周的聲望極高，都有被北周君王利用的價值，他們都一直無`法南歸，在北朝逝世。二十多年北朝同僚生活，兩者交誼，當是君子之交。

　　總之，庾信與王襃兩人，在四十歲左右遇到侯景之亂，投奔荊州江陵的蕭繹，本盼望即位的梁元帝蕭繹為中興之君，無奈元帝猜忌成性，梁室分崩離析，內鬥不止。庾信奉梁元帝之命出使西魏，任務未完成，江陵淪陷，梁亡。從此庾信不得南歸。王襃被俘入北，受到西魏宰相宇文泰禮遇，更受到北周明帝、武帝的重用，尤其武帝更看重他累世在江東為宰輔的政治經驗。王襃在北周有極高的政治地位。庾信成為北周文壇的領袖。梁末羈北文士以庾、王成就最高，影響最大。

　　㈢唱和之作

　　庾信與王襃在南朝梁時是梁皇太子蕭綱文學集團的文學侍從，從文獻中無法得知兩人有相互唱和之作。但侯景之亂後，兩人分別投奔在荊州江陵的梁元帝，成為蕭繹荊州文學集團文學侍從，兩人有唱和之作。據《周書、王襃傳》記載：「襃曾作〈燕歌行〉，妙盡關塞寒苦之狀，元帝及諸文士並和之，而競為淒切之詞。」38。當時「諸文士」之一便是庾信。王襃身處荊州爭戰之地，以其敏識多感而有此「淒切之詞」，其詞如下：

　　　　初春麗日鶯欲嬌，桃花流水沒河橋。

薔薇花開百重葉，揚柳拂地數千條。

隴西將軍號都護，樓蘭校尉稱嫖姚。

自從昔別春燕分，經年一去不相聞。

無復漢地關山月，唯有漠北薊城雲。

淮南桂中明月影，流黃機上織成文。

充國行軍屢築營，陽史討虜陷平城。

城下風多能卻陣，沙中雪淺詎停兵。

屬國小婦猶年少，羽林輕騎數爭行。

遙聞陌頭採桑曲，猶勝邊外胡笳聲。

胡笳向暮使人泣，長望閨中空佇立。

桃花落地杏花舒，桐生井底寒葉疏。

試爲來看上林雁，應有遙寄隴頭書。〈燕歌行〉

　　這首詩寫於梁元帝承聖二年（西元五五三年）左右，當時庾信正在江陵，庾信便與王褒有此唱和之作，其詞如下：

代北雲氣晝昏昏，千里飛蓬無復根。

寒雁邕邕渡遼水，桑葉紛紛落薊門。

晉陽山頭無箭竹，疏勒城中乏水源。

屬國征戍久離居，陽關音信絕能疏。

願得魯連飛一箭，持寄思歸燕將書。

渡遼本自有將軍，寒風蕭蕭生水紋。

妾驚甘泉足烽火，君訝漁陽少陣雲。

自從將軍出細柳，蕩子空床難獨守。

盤龍明鏡餉秦嘉，辟惡生香寄韓壽。

春分燕來能幾日，二月蠶眠不復久。

洛陽遊絲百丈連，黃河春冰千片穿。

桃花顏色好如馬，榆莢新開巧似錢。

蒲桃一杯千日醉，無事九轉學神仙。

定取金丹作幾服，能令華表得千年。〈燕歌行〉

　　庾信這首詩與王褒〈燕歌行〉可謂同曲同工，其對北風之傾慕似尤過之。於此可知在江陵時庾、王在蕭繹文學集團相互以詩會友。另有唱和之作者，在江陵之役，梁亡，兩人分別成為北周的臣子，庾信有〈忝在司水看治渭橋〉[39]，王襃和詩為〈和庾司水修渭橋〉[40]。庾信在北周閔帝宇文覺元年（西元五五七年）庾信封臨清縣子，食邑五百戶，初任司水下大夫，〈忝在司水看治渭橋〉詩，即寫在此時。詩曰：

　　　大夫參下位，司職渭之陽。
　　　富平移鐵鎖，甘泉運石梁。
　　　跨虹連絕岸，浮黿續斷航。
　　　春洲鸚鵡色，流水桃花香。
　　　星精逢漢帝，釣叟值周王。
　　　平堤石岸直，高堰柳陰長。
　　　羨言杜元凱，河橋獨舉觴。〈忝在司水看治渭橋〉

　　司水下大夫職務官品不高，但這是庾信入北周，朝廷對他重用的一份實職，因此這詩就生動地表現了他此時的心情。而王襃的〈和庾司水修渭橋〉則別有心情，其詩曰：

　　　東流仰天漢，南渡似牽牛。
　　　長堤通甬道，飛梁跨造舟。
　　　使者開金堰，太守擁河流。
　　　廣陵候濤水，荊峽望陽侯。
　　　波生從胡舶，沙漲湧新洲。
　　　天星識辨對，檢玉應沉鉤。
　　　空悅浮雲賦，非復採蓮謳。〈和庾司水修渭橋〉

　　總之，關於庾信與王襃有唱和之作，在文獻上所記載者：一是在荊州江陵的邊塞詩〈燕歌行〉。另一首是在西魏禪讓北周閔帝宇文覺時，庾信作〈忝在司水看治渭橋〉，王襃有〈和庾司水修渭橋〉詩。

　　庾信、王襃年輕時出生在南朝梁武帝時代，仕宦得意，平步青雲。壯年後，武帝晚年溺於佛教，荒於政事；又想投機，欲利用東魏降將侯景北伐，卻為侯景識破梁朝之空虛，而引發了侯景之亂；此亂遍及江東全境，餘波禍及江陵，未機即有江陵之禍，世家大族，再遭劫難。庾信與王襃便在歷史的無奈下先後相繼被迫羈北，屈仕西魏，再仕北周，一直無法南歸，兩人在北周：王襃在政治上頗有地位；庾信在北周文壇上獨享盛名。兩人從南朝梁都

是梁皇太子蕭綱文學集團的文學侍從；在江陵時又爲荊州蕭繹文學集團文學
侍從。兩人唱和之作，有據可考者唯有在江陵的〈燕歌行〉，入北的作品有
庾信〈忝在司水看治渭橋〉，王褒集中有〈和庾司水修渭橋〉等作品。從兩
人經歷與際遇中知道他們是同命同運，尤其羈北更是相憐相知，從庾信悼王
褒詩〈傷王司徒褒〉中可感受到這份眞情。

參、結語

　　庾信與王褒同是出生南朝梁武帝時代，由於國難，到江陵成爲同事，北
遷後又成爲羈北之臣。王褒於北周武帝建德五年（西元五七六年）左右，死
於宜州刺史任內，享年六十四歲。王褒之死，對庾信打擊強烈，可從〈傷王
司徒褒〉一詩感受到，本詩先敘述王褒的祖先事跡，再從王褒的少年期開始
描述，直到梁朝亡國後到北方的過程，最後嘆詠「昔爲人所羨，今爲人所
憐。世途旦復旦，人情玄又玄。故人傷此別，留恨滿秦川。定名於此定，全
德以斯全。惟有山陽笛，悽余思舊篇。」對王褒之死感慨深遠，不僅悲哀王
褒之死，也悲哀自己。於此可見兩人之友情，少年在南朝梁所受的禮遇，中
年經過侯景之亂，西奔江陵成爲同事，在江陵，他們本指望梁元帝中興，不
幸反使梁亡。兩人不得已又屈仕北朝，此心此意非同病相憐者難以感受。庾
信在悼亡詩中沉痛地說：「故人傷此別，留恨滿秦川。定名於此定，全德以
斯全。惟有山陽笛，悽余思舊篇。」道出庾信因爲王褒之死，顯得更加孤寂
淒涼無助，他那壓抑吞吐之音，無形中增加這首詩的哀傷和複雜，自然流露
出兩人深厚多面的情誼。

【附　註】

註1：陳致平《中華通史》第三册〈台北市，黎明文化事業公司，民國 64 年 10 月出
　　　版〉頁 255-258。

註2：參見《周書》卷四十，〈列傳〉第三十三。《北史》卷八十三，〈列傳〉第七十
　　　一〈文苑、庾信傳〉：「時肩吾爲梁太子中庶子，掌管記東海徐摛爲左衞率，
　　　摛子陵及信爲抄撰學士，父子在東宮，出入禁闥，恩禮莫與比隆。旣有盛才，
　　　文並綺豔，故世號爲徐庾體焉。當時後進，競相模範，每有一文，都下莫不傳
　　　誦。」〈北史 1243〉藝文印書館據清乾隆武英殿刊本景印。

註 3：參見北周、庾信撰，清、倪璠注《庾子山集注》第一册〈注釋庾集題辭〉頁一，
〈台北市，台灣中華書局印行，民國 69 年 11 月台版〉。

註 4：參見《隋書》卷五十八，〈列傳〉第二十三〈魏澹傳〉頁 7021。

註 5：參見譚繼山`篇編《望鄉詩人—庾信傳記》〈台北市，萬盛出版有限公司，76 年〉
頁 162。

註 6：同〈註 5〉頁 166。

註 7：同〈註 5〉頁 167。

註 8：同〈註 5〉頁 169-170。

註 9：同〈註 5〉頁 173-174。

註 10：關於王褒生卒年有各種考據：〈約 508-581〉，〈514？—575？〉，
〈 513-576〉等說法，本文採取日本學者清水凱夫《王褒傳記與文學》〈514—
577〉。

註 11：參見《周書》卷四十一，〈列傳 〉第三十三〈王褒傳〉頁 300。

註 12：蘇紹興著《兩晉南朝的士族》〈台北市，聯經出版事業公司，民國 76 年 3 月初
版〉頁 222。

註 13：參見《南齊書》卷二十三，〈列傳、王儉傳〉第四，頁 213。《南史》卷二十
二，〈列傳〉第十二。頁 277-278。

註 14：同〈註 11〉頁 300。

註 15：同〈註 11〉頁 300。

註 16：明、張溥《漢魏六朝百三名家集、後周王司空集題詞》頁 4919。

註 17：同〈註 2〉頁 302。

註 18：同〈註 12〉頁 222。

註 19：許東海著《庾信生平及其賦之研究》〈台北市，文史哲出版社，民國 73 年 9 月
初版〉頁 13-14。

註 20：呂光華《南朝貴游文學集團研究》〈政治大學中文系博士論文〉頁
220-228-229，238-248-249。

註 21：胡德懷《齊梁文壇與四蕭研究》〈南京市，南京大學出版，1997 年 7 月第一
版〉頁 6'8'9。

註 22：同〈註 2〉頁 302。

註 23：同〈註 20 〉頁 2'3'8。

註 24：同〈註 2〉頁 300。

註 25：同〈註 2〉頁 300。

註 26：楊家駱主編《新校資治通鑑注》〈台北市，世界書局，民國 61 年 11 月五版〉頁 4966。

註 27：同〈註 11〉頁 300。

註 28：同〈註 11〉頁 300。

註 29：同〈註 11〉頁 300。

註 30：參見《梁書》卷五〈本紀〉第五〈元帝〉頁 70。

註 31：同〈註 11〉頁 300。

註 32：同〈註 11,〉頁 300。

註 33：同〈註 11〉頁 300。

註 34：同〈註 11〉頁 301。

註 35：鄒萬紀著《魏晉南北朝史》〈台北市，眾文圖書公司，民國 79 年 6 月二版〉頁 95。

註 36：參見《隋書》卷七十八，〈列傳；庾季才傳〉第四十三：「武成二年，與王褒、庾信同補麟趾學士」頁 881。

註 37：鍾優民〈中國古代文學〉〈社會科學戰線，1986 ;12〉頁 58-65。

註 38：同〈註 11〉頁。

註 39：同〈註 3〉卷三。

註 40：同〈註 16〉頁 4946。

《聊齋志異》的仙妻形象與寓意

徐小梅

國防醫學院

人文及社會科學科講師

摘　　要

　　蒲松齡《聊齋志異》對仙凡婚戀題材的處理，堪稱後出轉精，超邁古人。無論是描寫天仙、謫仙、地仙或尸解仙與凡男締結姻緣，或凡男遊歷仙境與女仙成就姻好，無不用心經營，幻設敷寫，賦予豐富的文學旨趣與深厚的人間情味。作者通過對九位仙妻的形象塑造，表達了崇尚精神性靈的理念與維護親情孝道的立場，無疑兼具了仙道小說與儒家倫理的雙重性格。

　　關鍵詞：聊齋志異、蒲松齡、仙妻故事、翩翩、蕙芳、雲蘿公主、錦瑟、嫦娥、仙人島、粉蝶、白于玉、青蛾。

壹、前言

　　六朝志怪小說雖然以筆記小說的形式呈現，並以神仙妖鬼為表達對象，但在異類姻緣故事所表現的非常態的戀愛、婚姻關係，卻強烈地吸引有唐以降的文人，不斷翻空造奇，繼承發揚，及至清初的《聊齋志異》遂將此類故事的作品質量與藝術水準，同時推上了最高峰。根據統計，蒲松齡青睞於異類姻緣的題材是顯而易見的 1，這些「有意為之」的作品，不但使異類姻緣故事有了長足的進步，亦使鬼狐仙妖形象產生相當程度的質變。

　　就人仙婚戀題材而論，由於此類故事具有離奇曲折的故事情節，也易造成奇幻荒誕的審美效果，因而千餘年來不斷傳布，造成相當深遠的影響。以《太平廣記》為例，卷五十六至七十，共收「女仙類」故事約一百條，卻充斥著「昇天」的事蹟，太上老君出現頻繁，鍊丹服食的鏡頭亦不時可見，無疑瀰漫著道教的色彩。至於對女仙與凡男實質婚戀的描寫，則寥寥可數。如〈趙旭〉故事中趙旭與嫦娥女 2 或〈郭翰〉故事中郭翰與天上織女之間 3，雖有若干感情的著墨，故事情節主要聚焦在道教的神祕氣氛上，以突顯其神異事蹟；僅有〈楊敬眞〉4、〈裴玄靜〉5 等少數幾位守靜好道的女仙曾擁有短暫的婚姻生活。是故整體言之，女仙凡男的婚戀故事在《太平廣記》中，尚未臻至成熟。

　　反觀《聊齋志異》，涉及仙凡婚戀主題的作品，在作者蒲松齡悉心構思下，卻堪稱後出轉精，超邁古人。不過，學界始終缺乏細緻的探討與系統的研究，鑑乎此，本文擬採「主題研究」的方法，針對《聊齋志異》仙妻故事進行全盤考察，以期開掘蒲松齡深層的創作意圖與精神內涵。

貳、母題的界定與相關研究

　　由於仙女的身份特殊，仙女與凡男的締姻形式上不論私自締結姻好，或由尊長作主婚配，只要雙方有共同生活或同居之事實，即列爲討論對象。另外，因爲仙女傳統的絕情傾向，只要男女雙方均有共識，無論是否發生媾和關係，只要女方居於正室大婦的地位皆可視爲有效的婚姻。此外，仙女與凡男一宵歡好，期年後奉還一子，仍得視爲夫妻關係。

　　由於仙女，凡男活動的空間不同，一爲仙境，一爲人間，因此必須有一方離開原來的世界，才有締結姻緣的可能。因此根據故事發生的主要地點，可將仙妻故事（即人仙婚戀）分爲三種類型：

　　一、仙女下凡締姻

　　　　仙母遣派仙女下凡，婚配人間男子。

　　二、仙女謫降人間

　　　　仙女因罪謫入人間，促成仙凡締姻。

　　三、凡男遊歷仙境

　　　　人間男子進入仙境，幸得仙女爲妻。

　　近人針對六朝以降的人仙婚戀小說所做的分類，不時可見，卻大同而小異，與本文相關之研究包括：

　　一、賴芳伶《唐代異類婚戀小說研究》：將人仙婚戀區分爲仙凡巧遇，仙人降眞兩種型態6。

　　二、顏惠琪《六朝志怪小說異類姻緣故事研究》：將仙凡戀愛的題材略分為二類，一為仙鄉奇遇型，一為仙人降真型7。

　　三、周正娟《聊齋志異婦女形象研究》：將仙凡戀區分為二種型態，一為艷遇式，二為締姻式8。

　　四、姜素芬《中國傳統短篇小說仙妻故事研究》：歸納為三個類型，分別為仙女入人境──仙女下凡類型，仙女入人境──仙女轉世類型與凡男遊仙境9。

　　五、吳聖青《閱微草堂筆記》與《子不語》中兩性關係研究：分為人仙聯姻、仙人自降、凡人成仙、人求仙緣四種型態10。

　　上述相關論述，多注意分類研究，這些論點見仁見智，但都未能完備。以姜素芬搜羅之故事文本最為豐富，所做分類亦最為詳盡，其中雖涵蓋了《聊齋志異》，但未涉及人仙婚戀本身的內涵與仙妻形象的探討。為求通盤深入了解，必須進一步分析出最小的構成單位（即motif──情節單元），方能有助於理解《聊齋志異》仙妻故事類型的共同結構，並找尋作品之間的連繫11。

　　古人嚮往仙境，艱難求仙，莫不是為了長生不死，永世享樂，但仙界卻有明顯的等級之分。葛洪《抱朴子》中曾多次提及三品仙說，首見於〈論仙篇〉：

　　　按仙經云：上士舉形昇虛，謂之天仙；中士遊於名山，謂之地仙；下士先死後蛻，謂之尸解仙。12

　　在《聊齋志異》仙妻故事中，下凡締姻的仙女，始終保持「天仙」的尊貴身份，因罪謫人降人間的仙女，日後得視機緣重返仙界，謂之「謫仙」13；至於凡男遊歷仙境，締結姻緣的對象，皆為「地仙」。此一情形反映出蒲松齡對凡男與仙女之間的奇幻婚配，特多好感，遂一再敷寫。值得注意的是，蒲松齡對於「謫仙」與「地仙」的用心經營，賦予了豐富的文學旨趣與人間情味，惟前者與仙道類小說的宗教內涵是否類同14，又或後者與民間故事的基型15是否一致，仍有待按照「母題」一一分析《聊齋志異》相關作品，方能有所確定。

　　《說文解字》云：「讁，罰也。」可知「讁」是一種因罪而受罰的動作，仙女因觸犯戒律，讁入人間，往往必須隱藏眞實身份，靜待罪滿之後始可復返仙界，反映出道教中人以人世爲臭濁污穢的看法，此無非是以仙界的清淨聖潔所做的一種強烈對比，用以明顯區隔仙／凡、聖／俗、上界／下界、淨域／紅塵。16

　　分析唐前的讁仙傳說，已形成一深層結構：

一、某人名籍：多不言姓氏，或只稱某地之人。

二、出現情況：忽然出現，或舉止、職業多屬卑賤、不露眞相。

三、試煉歷程：擔任賤役，接受磨難，或肩負一些職責。

四、點破情由：由於某一機緣點破身份。

五、歸返天界：不知所終、尸解或直寫昇天。17

　　這一結構到了唐人手中並未變動，較具特色的是解說讁降情由，對命定說的強調、情緣的結與解18。至於《聊齋志異》「讁仙」類型的仙妻故事，基本上仍然遵循著「讁降──受難──回歸」的結構發展情節，惟描敘的重點大多集中於考驗的歷程，以極力舖寫讁仙與凡男歷經波折的結合過程，進而強調命定情緣觀念。其中，蒲松齡特重凡男人品的刻劃而賦予了新意，可視爲《聊齋志異》在「讁仙」類型故事的突破與創新。

　　《說文解字》仙作仚，「人在山上貌，从人从山。」可知在古人觀念中，仙人即是山中之人。而道教三品仙說中的地仙，多逍遙居停於名山之間，旣不遠離人間，又帶有脫俗超越的意味，正是仙境的理想典型。「地仙去留任意，適意自在，完全是漢晉之際隱遁思想的反映19。」所以葛洪也以爲地仙是最理想的仙品。

　　凡男遊歷仙境與女仙成就姻好，乃屬他界遊歷故事類型20。大致而言，自六朝以降，此類幻設的他界故事中，都有一固定的情節模式，即依循「出發──歷程──回歸」的基調進行21，蒲松齡在創作此類故事時，固然沿用了相同的結構形式，女仙的身份卻不限於地仙而已，天仙、尸解仙的身影亦曾驚鴻一瞥，無形之中擴大了女仙在這類故事活動的空間，情節的處理也更爲奇詭多變。

　　若試以小川環樹在從五十一個六朝仙鄉故事歸納所得的八項共通點即山中或者海上、洞穴、仙藥和食物、美女與婚姻、道術與贈物、懷鄉和歸鄉、時間，以及再歸與不能回歸等，進一步在稍後加以分析檢視，則可發現《聊齋志異》的凡男遊歷仙境故事也傳達出在現實生活裡無法滿足的理想22。無論是人跡罕至的山中洞穴，與世隔絕的海上仙島，或瑰麗恢奇的天界宮庭，遊歷者莫不經由接引而有仙境遇艷之情節，最後，都因懷鄉孝親而歸返現實世界。這樣的結局並不因爲凡男身份是否與道門相關有所不同，豈不令人玩味？

參、篇目的選定與情節提要

對於《聊齋志異》仙妻故事篇目，相關的論著頗有出入，略述如下：

陸又新認爲共有九篇：〈翩翩〉、〈蕙芳〉、〈仙人島〉、〈嫦娥〉、〈雲蘿公主〉、〈神女〉、〈織成〉、〈粉蝶〉、〈錦瑟〉。23

顏惠琪指出共有三篇仙鄉故事：〈翩翩〉、〈仙人島〉、〈青蛾〉24

姜素芬以爲共有七則：〈翩翩〉、〈蕙芳〉、〈仙人島〉、〈嫦娥〉、〈雲蘿公主〉、〈粉蝶〉、〈錦瑟〉。25

其中，〈神女〉實爲幽冥締姻26，而〈織成〉既爲唐人傳奇〈柳毅〉之苗裔，殆爲人神姻戀27。至於辜美高將〈仙人島〉列入狐篇，顯有不妥28，故從楊昌年說，將此篇故事歸爲仙29。

至於卷五〈白于玉〉篇，因具備凡男遊歷仙境情節，並因此一度春宵，復一舉得男，完全符合本文前述對仙妻之定義，自應予以列入討論。〈青蛾〉雖亦具備凡男遊歷仙境情節，惟發生於仙凡締姻，儷愛八載並育有一子之後，甚爲特殊。青蛾瘞一竹杖，尸解成仙，後霍生迷途荒竄間，誤入仙府與岳父力爭，方得與青蛾連袂返回人間，重續姻緣。惟疑因故事情節奇峭曲折，致遭人忽略，本文亦擬一併列入討論。以下即分別按照前述仙妻故事的三種類型分析其情節母題。

一、仙女下凡締姻類型，僅得〈雲蘿公主〉一篇：

凡男	仙女	初降	阻礙	降詰	婚姻生活	媾合	相處時間	生養子嗣	暫別	結局
安大業士子年十六，（未婚）溫文誠信	雲蘿公主聖后遣令公主下嫁	一日安獨坐公主扶婢肩入宅。	生急於落成無暇禁忌刻日敦迫，廊舍一新，遂犯天刑。	君不信數，遂使土木爲災，是急之而反以得緩。	兩情相悅，棋酒同歡	✓	六年	二子	忽辭生，欲後暫歸寧，至寧期不來。積年餘，音信全渺。	歸又不復返。

二、仙女謫降人間類型，共得〈蕙芳〉、〈嫦娥〉、〈錦瑟〉三篇：

篇名	蕙芳	嫦娥	錦瑟
地點	青州	廣陵	沂水
凡男	馬二混 貨麵爲業 家貧無婦 樸訥誠篤	宗子美 士子 年十四（未婚） 溫婉如處子	王生 士子 年十九（已婚） 風標修潔樸誠廉謹
仙女名籍	蕙芳 問其姓氏，曰：「母肯納我，我乃言，不然，固無庸問。」	問其小字，則名嫦娥。	婢曰：「小字錦瑟，東海薛候女也。」
出現情況	一日，忽有美人來，嫗驚顧窮詰，女笑曰：「我以賢郎誠篤，願委身母家。」	先是嫗獨居，女忽自至。	婢曰：「娘子慈悲，設給孤園，收養九幽橫死無歸之鬼。」
試煉歷程		夜方熟寢，女急起，驚言盜入，一人掠嫦娥負背上闃然而去。宗大悲，惝然失圖，荏苒三四年，鬱鬱常不聊賴。	婦尤驕倨，常庸奴其夫，生二度含憤出，欲覓死。願在地下服賤役，積兩年餘。
點破身分	積四五年，忽曰：「我謫降人間十餘載，因與子有緣，遂暫留止，今別矣！」	女曰：「實相告，妾實姮娥被謫，浮沈俗間，其限已滿，託爲寇劫，所以絕君望耳。」	「實告君，妾乃仙姬，以罪被謫，自願居地下，收養冤魂以贖帝譴。」
婚姻生活	兩情相悅	兩情相悅，歌舞助興	相敬如賓
媾合	∨	×	×
相處時間	四五年	終生	三十年
生養子嗣	無子女	一子一女	無子女（仙婢春燕生一子，妾生二男二女）
歸返天界	女曰：「請別擇良偶，以承盧墓，我歷月當一至。」已忽不見。 後三年，七夕，女忽入，以兩相依依，語無休止。忽空際有人。呼蕙芳，女急起，言已遂逝。	×	「居三十年，女時反其家……一日，攜婢去不復來。」

三、凡男遊歷仙境類型，共得〈翩翩〉、〈粉蝶〉、〈仙人島〉、〈白于玉〉、〈青蛾〉五篇：

篇名	仙女／凡男	仙鄉		人仙接遇原因	引入者	婚姻生活	媾合	相處時間	生養子嗣	懷鄉與歸鄉	結局
翩翩	翩翩	山中	洞穴	無心邂逅	翩翩	兩情相悅	✓	十五年	生一子教兒讀	「以故里，叔老為念」	「後生思翩翩，偕兒往探之。黃葉滿徑，洞口雲迷，零涕而返。」
	羅子浮										
粉蝶	粉蝶	海上	神仙島	船難	虛舟、仙婢粉蝶	兩情相悅		廝守終生	無子女	「家中懸念」	與轉世謫降之仙女締姻
	陽曰旦瓊州士人										
仙人島	芳雲	海上	仙人島	眞仙招遊天闕，下墮海島，再劫	道士崔眞人、仙婢明璫	詩文風雅「房幃之內，猶相愛好」	✓	廝守終生	無子女（王勉前妻育有一子）	「親老子幼，每切思懷」	凡男悟道，雙雙仙去「舍宇全渺，不知所在。」
	王勉中原才子										
白于玉	紫衣仙女	天上	天界	遊歷天庭，大開眼界	白于玉	（另娶葛女，絕情於燕好）	✓	一夜	不婚生子	×	凡男慕道，離家修道。成仙。
	吳筠知名士子										
青蛾	青蛾	山中	仙府	母病購魚、山中遇叟指點	道士、叟	兩情相悅	✓	三十年	生二子	×	仙女慕道，尸解成仙。凡男遊仙境夫妻同返人間。雙雙仙去。
	霍桓神童										

肆、人物的塑造與形象寓意

一、容貌絕美

　　仙女不比凡胎俗骨，蒲松齡運用輕描淡寫的印象主義筆法，交待女主角的出場，自有一種美得令人不敢逼視的驚艷效果，益增女主角一份神祕朦朧之美，一方面十分切合其異類身份，另一方面亦予讀者極力想像之空間 30：

　　　　服色容光，映照四堵。〈雲蘿公主〉

　　　　光艷明媚，若芙蕖之映朝日。〈仙人島〉

　　　　年可十六七，椎布甚樸，而光華照人。……睹之若仙。〈蕙芳〉

　　年十四五，飄灑艷麗。〈粉蝶〉

　　容貌若仙。〈翩翩〉

　　乃二十許天人也。〈錦瑟〉

　　殊色也。〈嫦娥〉

　　年十四五，美異倫常。〈青蛾〉

　　風致翩翩，……絕世者。〈白于玉〉

二、閒情風雅

　　相對於凡塵生活的辛勤與忙碌，仙家生活則象徵悠然與自適。人間原本平凡無奇的娛樂生活一旦被安置其中，就會在原有的休閒性之外益添暇趣。據研究，棋大盛於魏晉，下棋遂成為高人的雅事象徵31。棋局具鬥智性，有輸有贏，但〈雲蘿公主〉中，勝負之間卻洋溢著閨房樂趣：

　　　　安故好棋，楸枰嘗置坐側，一婢以紅巾拂塵，移諸案上曰：「主日耽此，不知與粉侯孰勝。」安移坐近案，主笑從之，甫三十餘著，婢竟亂之，曰：「駙馬負矣！」歃子入盒曰：「駙馬當是俗間高手，主僅能讓六子。」乃以六黑子實局中，主亦從之。……局闌未結，小鬟笑云：「駙馬負一子。」婢進曰：「主惰宜且退！」

　　〈嫦娥〉中，宗子美娶仙女嫦娥為妻，以狐女顛璫為妾，兩人親如姐妹，故事因著墨於兩女動靜之間，皆善於摩倣嬉戲而饒富閨房情趣：

　　　　嫦娥善諧謔，適見美人畫卷，宗曰：「吾自謂如卿，天下無兩，但不曾見飛燕楊妃耳。」女笑曰：「若欲見之，即亦不難。」乃執卷細審一過，便趨入室，對鏡裝修，倣飛燕舞風，既又學楊妃帶醉，長短肥瘦，隨時變更，風情意態，對卷逼真。……宗喜曰：「吾得一美人，而千古之美人，皆在床闥矣！」……顛當私謂宗，吾能使娘子學觀音，宗不信，因戲相睹。嫦娥每趺坐，眸含若暝，顛當悄以玉瓶插柳，置几上，自乃垂髮合掌，侍立其側，櫻唇半啓，瓠犀微露，睛不少瞬。宗笑之。

　　〈仙人島〉中，中原才子王勉與仙女芳雲婚後，不忘婢女明璫，閨房夫婦對酌，王欲招明璫，芳雲不許，故意將《孟子‧梁惠王》斷錯句並竄改數字，竟成了不許丈夫同婢女幽會的打趣話。後王勉不聽芳雲語，與明璫偷情，導致「前陰盡腫，數日不癒」。芳雲但凝視王勉，秋水盈盈，朗若曙星。王勉自我解嘲說：「卿所謂『胸中正，眸子瞭焉。』」芳雲反唇相譏：

「卿所謂『胸中不正，則瞭子眸焉。』」王勉用典亦出《孟子・離婁》，以此語討好芳雲，被芳雲順手牽羊，反過來大開玩笑，蓋「眸」爲「沒」的俗音，「瞭子」則爲山東方言對男子性器官的諧稱。聖賢大道理成了夫婦間帶色情意味的戲謔，雙方引經據典，調笑攻防之中，芳雲屢次絕聖棄賢，化腐爲新，才韜確實過人。

三、幻術神通

蒲松齡在仙凡締姻故事中，不斷發揮其驚人的想像力與一流的創意，使得仙妻超異常人的能力，自然地展現在食衣住行的細節上，不但滿足了日常生活最基本的需求，從而也描繪了仙妻們對夫婿子媳無微不至的呵護：

> 芳雲出素練一疋，望南拋去，化爲長堤，其闊數丈，瞬息駛過，堤亦漸收。……下車取籃中草具，布置如法，轉眼化爲巨第。……〈仙人島〉

> 女取山葉呼作餅，食之，果餅，又剪作雞魚烹之，皆如眞者。室隔一覽，貯佳醞，輒復取飲，少減則以溪水灌益之。……翩翩乃翦葉爲驢，令三人跨之以歸。〈翩翩〉

> 馬喜，入室見翠棟雕梁，伴於宮殿中之，几屏簾幃，光耀奪視，……天明出門，則茅廬依舊，……笥中貂錦無數，任馬取著，而出室門，則爲布素，但輕煖耳。〈蕙芳〉

> 生得女，意願已慰，不復置辯，但憂路陰難歸，女折兩枝，各跨其一，即化爲馬，行且駛，俄頃至家。〈青蛾〉

四、預知未來

仙女與凡男締姻後，爲人妻爲人母，最放心不下的，莫過於夫婿的生死與兒女的婚配，一如凡間婦女。值得注意者，她們雖具有預知未來的異能，卻都遵行命數，順乎自然，而未加強求：

> 女曰：「子壽八旬，至期我來收爾骨。」〈蕙芳〉

〈雲蘿公主〉中，公主與安大業育有二子，長子福相，因名大器，後果眞「十七歲及第，娶雲氏，夫妻皆孝友。」次子則不然，曰：「豺狼也。」立命棄之，生不忍而止，名曰可棄，囑生曰：「記取四年後，侯氏生女，左脅有小贅疣，乃此兒婦，當婚之，勿較其門地也。」果然在其預作警示下，可棄覓得良妻，終得走上正道。

五、穿越時空

蒲松齡筆下的仙妻，自由來去人間仙界，或因任務在身，或因戀戀娘家，雖擺脫了時空的侷限，來去自如，卻擺脫不了「人生離合，皆有定數」的安排：

> 婢出一物，狀類皮排，就地鼓之，雲氣突出，俄頃四合，冥不見物，索之已杳。……忽辭生，欲暫歸寧，積年餘，才返回人間。從此一年半歲，輒一行，往往數月始還，生習爲常亦不之怪。又生一子，後又歸寧，不復返。〈雲蘿公主〉

> 女時反其家，往來皆以夜。一日，攜婢去不復來。〈錦瑟〉

> 已忽不見，……後三年，七夕，女忽入，……忽空際有人呼蕙芳，女急起，……言已遂逝。〈蕙芳〉

〈蕙芳〉故事末尾，異史氏曰：「馬生其名混，其叢褻，蕙芳奚取哉？于此見仙人之貴樸訥誠篤也。余嘗謂友人：若我與爾，鬼狐且棄之矣，所差不愧于仙人者，惟混耳。」蒲松齡將馬二混與自己作了比較，認爲馬二混所具有的樸訥誠篤也是他自己所具有的品質，因而他也可以無愧于仙人。仙人既能屈尊下顧馬二混，又何嘗不能屈尊下顧他蒲松齡呢？儘管他解嘲似地自稱「鬼狐且棄之」，實際上的不勝歆羨之情已溢于言表。據此，蒲松齡在創作仙妻故事時，不無可能把自己的婚姻生活中，因爲幕賓和坐館而不得不長期忍受孤寂無聊，壓抑情愛的心理，轉化爲奇幻動人的故事，並從而投射了個人美好的願望。

《聊齋志異》中，勇敢追求，大膽行動的女性人物，大多是超自然的異類，相較於幽靈精怪可以完全按照自己的感受去愛去恨，蒲松齡筆下的仙妻反而受到相當的社會傳統、道德規範的限制。顯示「蒲松齡在婚戀問題上是一個保守的自由婚姻的擁護者，擁護自由婚戀的保守派。」[32] 更進一步地說，蒲松齡對仙妻的塑造，儘管在容貌、個性、異能皆符合道教化的女仙形象，然而細加玩味，她們其實相當程度地反映了作者維護儒家價值的立場與用心。以下試分別探究之。

一、價值觀

(一)重視誠篤

「馬二混，以貨麵爲業，家貧，無婦，與母共作苦。……守窮廬，日得蠅頭利，僅足自給。」卻偏能得到仙女蕙芳的青睞，願委身母家。蕙芳揀擇良善老實的凡間男子為侶，自有超越世俗的價值觀，她珍視的是馬二混的「誠篤樸訥」的美德，她用心良苦保護的也正是馬二混渾似璞玉的內在美質。

　　無獨有偶，天上聖后屬意凡男安大業「溫文誠信」，故遣府中雲蘿公主下降人間，自來相就。至於因婦驕倨而自願在地下服賤役的王生，之所以因禍得福，得到神仙美眷錦瑟，亦因其兩年餘來工作表現始終「誠樸廉謹」之故。可見《聊齋志異》中的仙妻故事，將誠篤列為最優先的擇偶條件，殆無疑義，充分顯示蒲松齡重視人品的觀念。

　　㈡棄絕功名

　　〈雲蘿公主〉中，蒲松齡借雲蘿公主之口說：「烏是儻來者為？無足榮辱，止折人壽數耳。三日不見，入俗幛又深一層矣。」事實上，安大業之所以幾墮入科考之俗幛中，完全是因為公主產下長男大器後，「忽辭生，欲暫歸寧，問返期，答以三日，至期不來，積年餘，音信全渺，亦已絕望。生鍵戶下幛，遂領鄉薦，終不肯娶。」生在公主逾期未歸，芳蹤杳然之際，將滿腔的思念與一心的等待完全轉注在閉門苦讀上，原以為公主聽聞秋捷必喜，不料公主竟視科考功名為浪費生命，「生由是不復進取。」

　　〈仙人島〉中的王勉，在仙鄉數十寒暑後，重返人間。目睹故居已屬他姓，田產已被不肖子賭賣一空，母妻皆已物故，老父衰朽堪憐。王由是萬念俱灰：「王初歸時，尚有功名之念，不愜於懷；及聞此況，沈痛大悲，自念富貴縱能攜取，與空花何異？」

　　人生的荒誕感油然興起，王勉因而擺脫了先前無法擺脫的科舉羈絆。身為士子，這曾是他生命依託之處，現在終於越出了社會的常軌。作為兒子，卻仍然牽腸掛肚，難以棄絕。對於王勉內心的痛苦，芳雲默默提供了毫無保留的精神支持與金錢後援。在蒲松齡的筆下，凡夫難與所來自的家庭一刀兩斷，總是依戀難捨，仙妻則表現出一種不即又不離，有情似無情的態度。前者在出世入世上的猶疑徘徊，後者在仙境人間之間來去自如，也恰巧對照驗證了仙凡之別。似乎說明了這些凡夫唯有處在生命意識覺醒之際，才有可能出現人生態度的根本轉向。

二、道德觀

㈠尊長作主

中國古代婚姻講究父母之命，媒妁之言，重視「門當戶對」，婚姻的當事人特別是女方毫無自由可言，清初門第尤其森嚴，蒲松齡卻通過〈翩翩〉仙女與浪蕩子羅子浮山中洞府結室生子的優美情節，〈蕙芳〉的女主角幻化為楊媼，自為媒與馬二混成婚的堅定行動，衝決對建禮教的束縛，竭力闡發她們的主體意識。不過《聊齋志異》的仙妻無論有否選擇婚姻的自主權，卻多由女方尊長作主，實與人間社會無異。

〈錦瑟〉中，謫仙錦瑟因附體之緣，主動表白欲結姻好，然無媒羞自薦，故請來長姐瑤台出面主婚，婚事始諧。可見錦瑟對婚事的儀式與名份慎重其事。

〈嫦娥〉中，謫仙嫦娥依附凡婦林媼，經其作主許婚，方得正式下嫁宗子美。兩人婚配亦因林媼的貪財毀約而一波三折。

〈粉蝶〉篇，仙婢粉蝶塵緣未盡，經主人十娘作主，貶謫轉世人間，投生作錢荷生，方與陽曰旦了卻宿緣。

㈡行止端莊

在中國古代文學中，嫦娥可稱為第一個敢於反抗男權婚姻的女性，《聊齋志異》中的嫦娥，似已與「嫦娥原型」的高傲孤峻，玄遠縹渺不同。蒲松齡筆下的嫦娥原本溫柔解語，待宗子美娶狐精顛當為妾後，嫦娥更持重不輕易諧笑，任由丈夫和顛當歡好，自己反樂得獨宿，僅在顛當過分輕佻，恐樂極生悲時，方以正室身分干涉，加以警告。「顛當憮然為間，忽若夢醒……由是閨閣清肅，無敢譁者。」

〈雲蘿公主〉中，「女無繁言，無響笑，與有所談，但俯首微哂。」某日，安大業欲令輕如嬰兒的公主作掌中舞，公主斷然拒絕曰：「此何難？但婢子之所為，不屑耳。飛燕原為九姊侍兒，屢以輕佻獲罪，怒謫塵間，又不守女子之貞，今已幽之。」此種寡言貞靜，端謹自持的美好形象，相當吻合傳統禮教的尺度要求。

三、倫理觀

㈠妻尊妾卑

《聊齋志異》仙妻故事中，雙美共事一夫的情形所在多有，譬如〈錦瑟〉中，錦瑟除主動爲丈夫物色美妾外，對納婢一事亦樂觀其成。〈嫦娥〉中，嫦娥做爲嫡妻端莊有禮，嫦娥與宗子美同居，只有夫婦之名，而不行夫妻繾綣之實。狐妾「顛當慧絕，工媚，嫦娥樂獨宿。」正室禁欲不育，寬容不妒，妾婢嚴守分際，彼此相安無事，凡男遂能坐享齊人之福，延續後代。可見嫡庶有序，妻妾相安，是蒲松齡表彰肯定的。

(二)生養子嗣

傳統社會中對於女人無子大多給予負面評價，所謂「不孝有三，無後爲大。」但《聊齋志異》仙妻凡夫的婚姻生活，部分改寫了「女人等於爲母」的腳本，如〈蕙芳〉、〈錦瑟〉及〈仙人島〉中的芳雲，均未生育，個中關鍵即在於她們爲自己的生育做出了主張。似乎是蒲氏有意把母職的意義與實踐，從生物性的生養關係開展出來，藉由不生育，顯現仙女逾越社會規範的器識。至於〈嫦娥〉中，「宗常患無子，嫦娥腹中忽聞兒啼，遂以刀刃破左脅出之，果男。無何，復有身，又破右脅而出一女。」這種令人嘖嘖稱奇的無性生殖方式，相當大膽地顛覆了接續宗祧的象徵意義，不妨視爲蒲松齡尊重女權的進步表現。

(三)親情爲先

〈仙人島〉、〈粉蝶〉的男主人翁入出仙境，猶不忘週全地照顧父母、家人，〈翩翩〉中，羅子浮在仙境洞府生活十數寒暑，依然心繫叔老，仙妻們也能予以體諒，不吝配合，顯示蒲松齡珍視的乃是入世情味濃厚的社會價值：

> 踰數月，王以親老子幼，每切懷思，以意告女。……王涕下交頤，哀與同歸，女籌思再三，始許之。桓翁張筵祖餞，……芳雲曰：「實與君言，我等皆是地仙，因有宿分，遂得陪從，本不欲踐紅塵，徒以君有老父故不忍違，待父天夫，須複還也。」……早旦，命王迎養。……驅馬至西村，見父衣服浑敝，衰老堪憐，相見，各哭失聲，王乃載父而還。芳雲朝拜已，燀湯請俗，進以錦裳，寢以香舍，又遙致故老，與之談讌，享奉過於世家。〈仙人島〉

〈翩翩〉中，翩翩具有情人、妻子、母親、婆婆的多重身份33，故事中爲人父的羅子浮因眷念叔老，屢次主動求歸，卻因翩翩愛子心切，而延宕再三。夫妻雙方立場各自不同，卻同出於親情人倫之考量。翩翩歷經生子、養子、教子、娶媳等心境之轉折，別有出世超塵的美感：

> 逾年，生一子，極慧美，日在洞中，弄兒爲樂，然每念故里，乞與同歸。女曰：「妾不能從，不然，君自去。」因循二三年，兒漸長，遂與花城訂爲姻好。生每以叔老爲念，女曰：「阿叔臘故大高，幸復強健，無勞懸耿，待保兒婚後，去住由君。」女在洞中，輒以葉寫書教兒讀，兒過目即了。女曰：「此兒福相，放教入塵寰，無憂不至臺閣。」未幾，兒年十四，花城親詣送女，女華妝至，容光照人，夫妻大悅，舉家讌集，翩翩扣釵而歌曰：「我有佳兒，不羨貴官，我有佳婦，不羨綺紈。今夕聚首，皆當喜歡，爲行君酒，歡君加餐。」與兒夫婦對室君，新婦孝，依依膝下，宛如所生。生又言歸，女曰：「子有俗骨，終非仙品，兒亦富貴中人，可攜去，我不誤兒生平。」……翩翩乃翦葉爲驢，令三人跨之以歸。

四、命定觀

古人相信一切事物冥冥之中自有定數。仙女託言「有緣」，自薦於凡男，一方面對自己所作所爲予一合理解釋，不至過於唐突，另一方面，以此解釋生命中的聚散離合，也將使凡男易於接受，並安於仙女的安排。34《聊齋志異》仙妻故事通常由女方主導，當女方把一切委諸天意、夙分，意味著男女主角遇合的必然性，乃出自於一種超自然神祕力量的合理有意的安排。如此即平添了一層非世俗的神聖性，而不可更易。再者，仙女既來自仙界恐終將回返仙界，故命定論調可及早爲雙方未必白首廝守預作宣示。

> 過數月，又欲歸寧，生殊淒戀，女曰：「此去定早還，無煩穿望，且人生離合，皆有定數……。」〈雲蘿公主〉

> 忽曰：「我謫降人間十餘載，因與子有緣，遂暫留止，今別矣！」〈蕙芳〉

五、創作觀

蒲松齡自己說過：「景物俱可移情。」（〈我曰偶和詩·跋〉）在《聊齋志異》的仙妻故事中，作者有意且成功地將仙女活動的環境加以渲染描繪，創造奇幻迷離、仙凡殊異的藝術氛圍，以烘托人物的性格與形象。如〈粉蝶〉中，海上歷劫不死的陽生初入神仙島，面對眼前彷彿世外桃源的境域，自是無限好感，也爲故事情節的開展做好準備：

　　　　忽見島嶼，舍宇連互，把棹近岸，直抵村門。村中寂然，行坐良久，雞犬無聲。見一門北向，松竹掩靄，時已初冬，牆內不知何花，蓓蕾滿樹，心愛悅之。

　　反觀〈錦瑟〉篇，則通過王生眼中給孤園的陰森恐怖、污穢不堪，間接勾勒謫仙錦瑟在冥界甘心贖罪的堅毅形象：

　　　　移時，見一門，署給孤園。入見屋宇錯雜，穢臭熏人，園中鬼見燈群集，皆斷頭缺足，不堪入目。回首欲行，見尸橫牆下，近視之，血肉狼籍。

　　至於〈青娥〉篇，寫迷不可見的仙人所居山村是「夕暾漸墜，山谷甚雜，又不可以極望。……而山路崎嶇，不可復騎，跋履而上，昧色籠煙矣。」寫青娥所居仙府是「忽睹廊舍，並無紅燭，而光明若盡。」迷離眩目，前後呼應，益見仙凡之殊。

　　在《聊齋志異》仙妻故事中，描繪仙境之自由安適，最近似〈袁相根碩〉者，莫過於〈翩翩〉，亦恰與「翩翩」一詞的原義──自得自樂，貌美文雅，緊密扣合：

　　　　入深山中，見一洞府，入則門橫溪水，石梁駕之。又數武，有石室二，光明徹照，無須燈燭。

　　在這片天地之中，作者通過「餐葉衣雲」的奇想巧思，不但成功塑造了女主角的形象之美，並進而刻劃了輕薄兒羅子浮身心淨化，蛻變成熟的過程。35 蒲松齡設境、造型的功夫，俱稱一流，顯示了進步的創作觀。

伍、結　語

　　在蒲松齡的筆下，凡男對仙妻充滿了信賴、依戀，處於受照顧的地位而心甘情願，仙妻也因而顯示了母性的特質36，可謂《聊齋志異》的一種特別的現象。他顛覆了儒家文化中「男尊女卑」、「男主女從」的經典論述，但卻保留了《禮記‧昏禮》所強調的「夫婦有義」、「父子有親」的觀念，積極維護了倫理孝道。

　　神仙世界本講究脫離世間情，但蒲氏筆下的仙妻們卻是有情愛、情緒的。但明倫評〈嫦娥〉有云：「惟仙多情，亦惟仙能制情；惟仙真樂，亦惟仙不極樂；此則文之梗概也。」即指出此點。蒲松齡在〈小翠〉末尾，假借異史氏曰：「仙人之情，亦更深於流俗。」更主動表示了贊許控制情慾，以致中和的意見，強調了性需求的滿足並非婚姻最重要的因素，足以窺見蒲松齡崇尚精神性靈的理念。

　　綜言之，《聊齋志異》的仙妻故事，兼具了仙道小說與儒家倫理的雙重性格，作者亦通過了仙妻的形象塑造，表現了鮮明的人格理想與婚戀觀念。

【註　釋】

註 1：陸又新撰：《聊齋志異中的愛情》（台北：台灣學生書局，1992 年 5 月），頁 18-20。

註 2：宋・李昉撰：《太平廣記五百卷》（台北：新興書局），第二冊，六十八，頁 426-428。

註 3：同前註，頁 442-443。

註 4：同註 2，頁 443-446。

註 5：同註 2，卷六十九，頁 454-455。

註 6：賴芳伶撰：《唐代異類婚戀小說研究》（台中：中興大學中文研究所碩士論文，1989 年），第四章第一節。

註 7：顏惠琪撰：《六朝志怪小說異類姻緣故事研究》（台北：文津出版社，1994 年 5 月），頁 76-86。

註 8：周正娟撰：《聊齋志異婦女形象研究》（台中：東海大學中文研究所碩士論文，1995 年 6 月），P124-125。

註 9：姜素芬撰：《中國傳統短篇小說仙妻故事研究》（新竹：清華大學中文研究所碩士論文，1998 年 6 月），頁 2-3。

註 10：吳聖青撰：《閱微草堂筆記與子不語中兩性關係研究》（台北：文化大學中文研究所碩士論文，2001 年），第四章。另可參看第二章第一節，又將夫妻感情分類為：兩情相悅類、天定姻緣類。

註 11：參見全榮華，《六朝志怪小說情節單元分類索引》（甲編）（台北：文化大學中文研究所，1984 年），頁 84-85。

註 12：晉・葛洪撰：《抱朴子》（台北：商務印書館，1939 年），卷二，冊一，頁 27。

註 13：謫仙的說法參見李豐楙撰：《誤入與謫降》（台北：台灣學生書局，1996 年 5 月），頁 20-21。

註 14：參見李豐楙撰：《六朝隋唐仙道類小說研究》（台北：台灣學生書局，1997 年 2 月），頁 8-9。

註 15：參見藤田佑賢撰：〈聊齋志異與民間說話〉，收《國際聊齋論文集》（北京：北京師範學院出版社，1992 年 7 月），頁 247。

註 16：參見李豐楙撰：《罪罰與解放：鏡花緣的謫仙結構研究》，《中國文哲研究集刊》，第七集，頁 144。

註 17：本文援引李豐楙撰：〈道教謫仙傳說與唐人小說〉一文之分析，收錄於其著《誤入與謫降：六朝隋唐道教文學論集》（台北：台灣學生書局，1996 年 5 月），頁 258。

註 18：同前註。

註 19：引自李豐楙撰：〈神仙三品說的原始及演變〉，刊於《漢學論文集》二，（台北：文史哲出版社，1973 年），頁 71-224。

註 20：他界仙鄉之說參小川環樹著，張桐生譯：〈中國魏晉以後的仙鄉故事〉，《中國古典小說論集》第一輯（台北：幼獅文化，1975 年），頁 85-95。

註 21：引自李豐楙撰：《探求不死》（台北：久大文化股份有限公司，1987 年 9 月），頁 107。

註 22：同註 20。

註 23：同註 1，頁 19。

註 24：同註 7，頁 231-232。

註 25：同註 9，頁 155。

註 26：「實告君，妾非人，乃神女也。家君為南岳都理司……。」又「家君感大德無以相報，欲以妹子附著婚姻，恐以幽冥見嫌也。」可知〈神女〉確為幽冥締姻。

註 27：參見董挽華撰：《從聊齋志異的人物看清代的科舉制度與訟獄制度》（台北：嘉新水泥公司基金會叢書，1976 年 9 月），頁 35-36。另可參見拙作〈聊齋志異與龍類故事〉，收《遠源學報》第十期，（1988 年 11 月），頁 96。

註 28：見辜氏〈談狐〉，《國際聊齋論文集》，頁 251-264。

註 29：見楊昌年撰：《聊齋志異研究》（台北：里仁書局，1996 年），第二章。

註 30：關於蒲松齡對異類女子的塑造，可參見梁伯傑〈聊齋女主角的塑造〉，《中國古典文學研究叢刊·小說之部·二》（台北：巨流圖書公司，1977 年 10 月），頁 181-188。

註 31：參見劉翔飛，《唐人隱逸風氣及其影響》，（台北：台大中文所碩士論文，1978 年），頁 69。

註 32：見安國梁撰：《聊齋釋眞》，（鄭州：中州古籍出版社，1993 年 11 月），頁 93。

註 33：過去對〈翩翩〉的探討，多注重翩翩與子浮的兩人情愛關係。（如郭玉雯、顏惠琪、陸正新、周正娟等人），卻未留意翩翩對子媳的關愛，尤其是翩翩愛子猶勝三分的強烈母性。

註 34：參見楊國樞〈中國人之緣的觀念與功能〉，收楊國樞主編《中國人的心理》，（台北：桂冠圖書公司，1970 年 4 月），頁 129-138。

註 35：參見郭玉雯：《聊齋志異的他界故事之研究》（台北：台灣大學中文研究所碩士論文，1982 年 6 月），頁 161-163。

註 36：參見劉惠華：《聊齋志異女性人物研究》（台北：台灣大學中文研究所碩士論文，1996 年），頁 131-132。

莊子的生命哲學

李開濟

國防醫學院

政治科學科副教授

摘　　要

莊子對於生命過程中的生死問題有三種看法：

1.循環論：生與死之交替如同晝與夜，四季自然的循環輪替，是不可避免的。

2.氣化論：萬物從無而有，又回歸於空無，只是一氣的形成變滅罷了。

3.解脫觀：大地承載著一切生物，養育之、成長之，辛勞度日、養家活口，老年時應得休息，死亡是澈底的歇下重擔，完全解脫。

關鍵字：大化、無用之用、螳螂捕蟬、死生一體、懸解、司命眞君

前言

莊子身處混亂殺伐的戰國時代，他歷經了貧困、喪妻、失業，潦倒不堪、借貸無門的窘境，然而他的思維很獨特，從風雨中飄搖的外境中，深刻洞察內在的心靈世界；在脆弱不堪一擊的生命懸絲上，他成就了自滿自足的超越之道。這種奇特的智慧爲中華文化豎立永遠的照明燈塔，至今不窮不絕。

本書在寓言體的《幽默禪》之後繼續探討莊子的奇特思想。《幽默禪》中並未論及莊子的思想與禪有何關係，只借用了「禪即智慧」這個概念；在續集《生命哲學》中將會進一步的考究莊子修養的方法，這套修爲方法在佛教中相當於辟支佛在山間林下獨自觀察大自然而悟道，非有師承脈絡，也無

派系傳承，而是獨自一人自省自悟得道的，這確實是禪法。屬於辟支佛的禪觀，獨創一格，空前絕後。

　　莊子對於人生的浮沈際遇有冷譏熱諷的應對，路見屍骨荒棄橫陳，有悲天憫人之情。他時時感嘆人生命運不可捉摸，也鞭闢入微剖析人性。在飽受無情困頓之後，不同於現代人的頹廢，他竟然形成一系列嚴格完整的修心養性之道，飄然出塵，指向神人、眞人、至人的性靈提昇。所以本書將從莊子的生死觀開始，欣賞莊子的洞察力，進而試圖了解無形的天命與抽象的人性，讓莊子精彩的智慧再次豐潤今日混亂的島國文化。

　　以下共蒐集莊子論及生死的十七則言論並作賞析。

一、貪生怕死

　　貪生怕死是一般人的反應，也是正常的心態。爲了增長世壽，有保養樂生的各種法子，吃、穿、花、用，花樣繁多；秦始皇企求不老仙丹就是一個例子。幾乎每一位君王享盡榮華富貴之後，心不滿足，還希望永遠長享盛世，子孫也繼續佔有江山。

　　莊子卻採用逆轉的方向來看：

　　＃我怎麼知道貪生死不是困惑呢？

　　　我怎麼知道怕死不是迷路忘返呢？

　　　我怎麼知道那些死去的人是否後悔生前的迷戀？＃

　　　　　　　　　　　　　　　　　　　　　　——齊物論

　　畏懼尙未發生的事是一種迷思；有人在家中坐，卻耽心牆外的野狗衝進來；有人外出，卻耽心家中財富遭人盜走。明明人還活著，又耽心死後草蓆裏屍太悽寒，就像艾封人的女兒麗姬尙未出嫁，卻哭哭啼啼怕的要命，遠離了父母家鄉，日後不知該怎麼辦？等嫁到晉國之後成爲王妃，天天穿金戴銀、吃香喝辣，幸福又美滿，才知道過去是白白耽心了。何苦害怕哭泣呢？

　　希臘哲人伊彼鳩魯教導學生：「死亡尙未發生，你怕什麼？若眞的死掉了，你反而不必害怕。反正死都死了，害怕也沒有用！」這是豁達，放得下。

　　自己糊塗了才貪生，以爲維持現狀才好，殊不知可能死後更好。莊子以麗姬出嫁前與後的心態作一對照，時間上呈現前後一直線，人是同樣一個人，心境不同罷了。

小時候外出，迷了路回不了家；死亡也有回歸之意，回到你原來的地方，怕死相當於迷路忘返，死亡才是回家，爲何害怕回老家呢？

死去的人可能自嘲當初的痴迷，死後解脫清淨又無負擔，不必養家活口，四處奔波遭罪。死後實在是享福，比生前好的太多。才知道過去太傻了，白白耽心死後的事。

伊彼鳩魯認爲：「旣生未死，不必耽心。旣死無知，更不必耽心。」這種說法屬於唯物思想的斷滅論：死後無知覺，死後無生命，所以不必耽心。唯物主義的斷滅論對於道德恐怕不能接受因果論，印度的卡耳瓦加派就是持斷滅論，主張只有現世，沒有未來；只要今生今世活的愉快，何必管它生前死後。因此在道德行爲上儘可爲所欲爲，反正不必耽心下地獄遭受果報。

莊子把生與死看成時間上的一條直線，如同夢時與醒時，婚前與婚後，這是類比式思考，實則生與死眞的在時空中一條直線上嗎？過去、現在、未來三時是彼此交融的，過去所發生的事件影響到現在，現在必然計劃將來，三時無形的相互交融影響，不可能只有現在不管將來，更何況生前與死後可能是二種不同的世界哩！死亡不但在時間上隔斷，空間上也屬於未知，形體上更是腐朽變形。所以直線式進行的只是時間，生命的複雜性包含的更廣，單向的直線序列不足以解釋生死問題。

二、安時處順

#老子李耳過世，好朋友秦失去弔問，只見他乾號三聲就離開了。

老子的徒弟們見了感到訝異，上前問秦失：

「您不是夫子的好朋友嗎？」

秦失答：「是呀！」

徒弟又問：「喂！那有人如此弔唁的？這麼簡慢！不合禮儀！」

秦失緩緩回答：「嗯！是這樣！起先我還以爲老子是位至人呢！其實不是。怎麼說呢？剛才我進去一看，有老年人在哭他，哭的好像自己的兒子死了一般；也有年青人在哭他，哀天嚎地的，像是自己死去了娘親！這些人之所以如此哀慟，一定有他們忍不住的因素，克制不住自己的情緒。這是違背天理，背叛眞性情啊！忘記了純眞的人性！以前的人稱它是違背天理的刑罰！遭此際遇有感而發，傷痛悲哀，啼泣不已，這些情緒上的折磨都是上天的懲罰！其實老子在世是他應有的時機；離去了也是順應天道。至人都是安天時、順天命的，符應天意，一切自自然然，何須傷感呢？承受天命的人喜怒哀樂無動於衷，哀樂不入於心；這種境界古人稱它為最高的解脫。」#

———養生主

　　哀樂不入於心叫做無動於衷，希臘哲學中的斯多噶學派也教人無動於衷，看透世情，無大悲大喜的激情，培養平靜的心情。

　　通常大善人生前付出甚多，所以死後廣受人民懷恩，若有鄰居為某位長者哭的有如喪子喪母一般，這足以證明死者一定生前恩德浩大，於民有澤，才能令人如此感念。在修道人秦失看來尚未脫俗離塵，算不得是「至人」。還在俗情恩惠中打混。老子沒有把其他人教會天道、天命、天時，沒有把親友訓練成喜怒哀樂不入於心的超然境地，不懂得安時處順、淡漠生離死別，所以悲哀之情正是上天的懲罰。

　　死亡，是該離去的時候！存活，是該有的機緣。怎麼來，怎麼去。如順應水流般，任運漂流，不必掙扎，不須強求，如四季花開葉落，何需輕彈淚珠兒呢？

　　安時處順，哀樂不能入，這是心獄的解脫。

　　死亡是完整生命的一部份。來、去、進、出，都是天道的展現，生有何歡？死又何感？平等待之則省卻許多不必要的干擾。

三、善生善死

　　莊子從人類的生死現象挖掘出背後隱藏的不可抗拒力，追溯宇宙的玄妙深意，從人生現象上升至宇宙論，進而相信冥冥之中有一位造物主，中國人稱之曰：「造化」，猶如工匠、冶鍊鋼鐵的鑄劍師。從生死現象探討背後的命運，先天已被決定、不可測知的天意、乃至於生化來源的天道，面對這一切高深莫測的際遇，莊子培養出安時順命的灑脫態度。

　　#死生是註定的命運，外在自然界有晝、夜、冬、夏的循環，這些都是奇妙的天意安排！

　　大自然承載著我的身軀，讓我為生活辛勤奔波，勞動作務，老年時讓我休閒，消磨時日，最後讓我死亡休息，這一切都是上天的旨意！所以珍惜生命的人既愛護生活的快樂幸福，也重視將養休息的衰老死亡。

子祀、子輿、子犂、子來四個人共同約定：

「誰能夠以虛無爲頭、以生爲背脊、以死爲尾椎，視生死存亡爲一個整體的，我們就跟他做朋友。」四人相視而笑，莫逆於心，彼此成爲知交。

不久子輿生病，子祀去看望他，子輿有感而發：

「偉大的造物主把我整的如此萎靡不振！彎腰駝背、五官朝上翻、下巴縮到肚臍裡、肩膀高聳、髮髻朝天、披頭散髮！」

子輿的病體陰陽不調，雖然生理有病，但心裡卻很閒適，他邁著蹣跚的步伐走到院子裡，對著井水看自己的倒影說：

「唉呀！造物者還以爲能困得住我呢！」

子祀問他：「你不喜歡這樣？」

子輿微微笑道：「噢！不是！我才不會嫌惡呢！假如上蒼把我的左手臂變化成公雞，我就會用它凌晨報曉；如果上蒼把我右手臂變化成彈弓彈丸，我就用它打小鳥烤來吃；要是造物者把我的尾椎變成車輛，心神變成一匹馬，那我就乘著馬車，四處遊歷，不用另尋車輛了！人生有得有失，高低起伏不斷；得，只是一時的際遇；失，也不過是順勢而爲。安時處順，就減少不必要的哀傷了！這種心境就是古時修道人所嚮往的解脫束縛之境；人之所以不能自我解脫，就是因爲受到外在物質的牽絆，然而一切外在物質都不久長，我又何必嫌惡什麼呢？」

接著子來有病，氣喘噓噓，快要死了！他的妻子兒女圍繞在床畔，耽心的哭泣流淚。子犂去他家慰問，看到這種哀悽的景象很不高興，叫他們走開：「去！去！去！都出去！讓病人靜養，別吵他。」

停息一會兒之後，子犂靠在臥室門邊與子來閒聊：

「偉大的造化！這會兒祂打算怎樣？不知祂要你做什麼？成爲小老鼠的肝臟？還是要你當一隻小蟲的胳臂？」

子來熙怡微笑說：「子女對父母親要唯命是從，大自然與人類的關係也相當於父子關係。若是大自然要我靠近死亡，而我反抗拒絕，那就是強悍不從，怨不得上天！大自然供給我的形軀，要我爲生活奔波勞累；要我在老年時休養，給我死亡以休息，所以既愛惜生命也愛惜死亡！生與死是完整一體的！如果有位鐵匠在鑄金時，一塊金屬跳出來對他說：『把我造成名劍鏌琊！』這位鐵匠一定以爲這塊金屬是妖孽，是不祥之金。同樣，上天在造化人類時，某一生靈叫著說：『我要當人類。』造化者也一定會認爲這是個妖怪，不吉祥的人，現在我把整個宇宙天地當作一只生命的大洪爐，以造化者爲鐵匠，隨便祂要怎麼鑄造我！變成蟲子也好，變成老鼠也好，隨祂的意吧！」子來接著安祥的入睡了，隔天醒來疾病反而去了大半，精神很好。

——大宗師

莊子有生命蛻變的想法，這不同於印度的輪迴觀，輪迴思想包含業力論、果報說，莊子思想中只有變化說，沒有業報論。

完整的觀察生命：生、老、病、死是萬事萬物發展的固定階段，樹木發芽、成長、落葉、結果，乃至於被砍伐、被雷電劈擊，人類無論貧富貴賤、壽長壽短，都有生死現象，往好處看，往積極面看，老年人體力衰弱，就不必再負擔養家活口的工作，留給兒孫去做；每一階段都有應當做的事。死亡有它的正面意義，讓人好好的休息！莊子有時會突發奇想：身體四肢變成其他東西，左手變成公雞，右手變成彈弓，或者縮小成爲蟲子、老鼠……。這是「物化」的思維，不是輪迴論，「物化」沒有理由，毫無規則可言，完全聽憑上天的旨意！有一點「不可知論」的味道。

把宇宙天地視作造化的大洪爐，放棄自我意志，任憑大化流行，表示死後仍然有生命存在，生命是不斷不滅的。這種信念莊子未再進一步分析，只把一切命運交托給茫茫蒼天！雖然對大化造物者不夠瞭解，卻深信死後仍然有生命存續，只是形體不同罷了。

四、生爲累贅，死爲決癰

#子桑戶、孟子反、子琴張，三個人共同商量：

「誰能與不往來交朋友？誰能爲無爲？事無事？誰能登上青天？遨遊於雲霧之中？精神振奮於無極之境？忘卻生命的一切干擾，超越於無限無窮之外？」三人相視不語，默契於心，成爲莫逆之交。

過不久子桑戶死了，尚未下葬，孔子聽到這個消息後，派遣最擅長外交辭令的子貢去協助喪事。子貢來到喪家，看不見慘淡景象，卻看到孟子反和子琴張在鼓琴唱歌，還搖頭幌腦地編寫輓歌曲調，吟哦推敲不已。這二個人唱著：

「唉呀！桑戶哪！唉唉喲！桑戶呀！

你已經返回天真自然之鄉了！

我們卻還在這兒受苦受難的做人！」

子貢聽了很不是味道，打抱不平的上前質問：

「你們對著死者的屍體唱歌，合乎禮教嗎？」

孟子反和子琴張二人嘻嘻一笑，反唇相譏說：「嘿！你懂的什麼是禮教？」

子貢碰了一鼻子灰回去，告訴孔子今天發生的怪事，並憤憤然說：「這二個人是誰？真不懂禮貌！放浪形骸，對屍而歌，一點兒也不哀傷，還嬉皮笑臉的！真不知該用什麼話來罵他們，這二人真怪。」

孔子嘆了一口氣，緩緩分析道：

「這兩個人是遊於方外的，不接受傳統禮教的束縛，我們儒者卻是遊方於內，接受世俗常情的約束，拘謹於世俗禮教。他們與我們相比，一者世俗，一者離俗，方內與方外，根本完全不同，我派你作代表去弔唁子桑戶是我的不對。我太孤陋寡聞了。方外之士與大自然造物者相偕為友，同遊於天地一氣；在他們的眼中生命是一種拖累，是個大疣包，死亡是回歸大自然，猶如剔除潰爛的膿腫瘡疽。生與死，死與生，生才是死！死才是生！生死之間誰先誰後呢？人身不過是五行物質的聚合，生命暫時寄託在肉身。方外之士早已忘記體內有五臟肺腑，也不在意外表有耳目五官；只是隨順著生命的波流任運變化，不必刻意計較始終端倪，讓精神渺陌，飄然出塵；心志逍遙於無為無意的境界，方外雅士豈會在乎世俗計較的煩瑣禮儀呢？他們更不可能為了別人的評價去遵守什麼禮法！」#

——大宗師

莊子提到「無為之業」，此業字不同於印度的業（Karma），印度的業有善業、惡業、非善非惡業，是由行為產生力量，力量造成後果，所以黑業感苦果，白業感樂果，強調內在蘊積的力量與作用；莊子的無為之業含義比較單純，只指作為、事業、無所為而為的一貫行徑。

生命過程中莊子感受苦難煎熬多於安樂幸福，從整個中國歷史來看，確實戰亂殺伐的年代遠超過承平盛世。看待莊子對生命有著深沈的悲哀，感覺生命是個重擔、累贅，所以渴盼結束不得已的拖磨。他迎接死亡，想結束這一切的不如意，好似醫生為病患破潰臃腫的膿瘡，清除了污血，痛苦才得減輕；至少死亡有一項好處：永遠擺脫塵世的勞苦。莊子不像一般人抗拒，反而以幽默感來為它加分！看待「死亡」為一個分離的客體，有其獨特的價值呢！

五、大化降臨

#顏回問孔子：「魯國的孟孫才最近以善居喪聞名於全魯，我去看過他家，也沒什麼特別的。他母親過世時，有哭聲，但無淚涕；面色正常，似乎內心平靜，沒什麼刺激或悲傷之感。在後院生活也一如往昔正常，沒有蛛絲馬跡的悲慟哀愁。他怎麼會得到善居喪的美稱呢？是否徒有虛名呀？我實在感到懷疑！」

孔子說：「孟孫才已經盡到應盡的本份了！而且還算得上是聰明的程度。只有在簡化形式上還做的不夠澈底，然而已經有所簡化了。以孟孫才來看，他不知人類為何有生命？也不知活的好好的為何會死？不知先生後死？還是先死後生？他的心境已經順應萬化，隨時等待大自然高深莫測的未來變化。再說死人不知活人事，活人不知死人事，生時不知死後事，死後忘記生前事，像我們兩人恐怕還在夢中，尚未覺醒哩。

孟孫氏的心境已經到了外在環境改變，但不影響內在心情的地步，四大色身如常運作，不妨礙心靈的純然平靜！孟孫才隨順常習，人哭亦哭，其實內心並不陷於哀傷。他尊重一般禮俗，內心不為所動！我們儒家所堅持的禮教難道一定真實必要嗎？你在晚上可以做夢，夢到自己是一隻飛鳥，飛翔於高空；也可以夢到自己是一條大魚，潛沈在江海深淵中；何者才是真實的呢？現在說話的人究竟是清醒還是在睡夢中？誰知道？個人心境獨特的體會，外表是顯現不出的，真正的熙怡也不是裝作刻意安排的。順應大自然的一切變化，才能與天道合一。」#

——大宗師

莊子多次提到夢，最出名的是莊周夢蝶，夢到自己是一隻蝴蝶，翩翩然在花園中遨遊；這兒夢到化身為鳥，遨翔於天空，無止盡的廣大青天任你雲遊暢快！也夢到化身為一條魚悠然江海，上可浮游於水，戲弄水草綠萍，下可沈潛海底深淵，波浪不興…。夢，看似虛幻，夢境中的覺受卻是真實深刻的！那種飛翔的感覺，無身體的重量，隨著意念變化，想去哪裡就去哪裡，不必一步一步走，只要腦海中有個意念就飛過去了。化身為魚也有特別的覺受，降入海底深淵是瞬間的下沈，快速又快速，來不及思考，剎那間思緒停頓；潛到水底世界，黑暗一片，安靜、無波、茫茫然，無邊無涯，廣大無止盡…。

夢境的感受很深刻、很真實、令人難忘。所以莊子才多處以夢境變化來譬喻，何者才真實？醒時是真？短暫的夢境才真？醒時是另一場大夢？有些人有「夢中夢」的經驗，誰知醒時不是另一場長夢？希臘畢達哥拉斯學派認為：出生是靈性的死亡，身體是靈魂的墳墓；死亡是靈魂的解脫，也是靈性的復甦。所以莊子質疑：不知誰先誰後？死先、生後？還是生先、死後？以天鄉的角度來看，落入塵世是靈性的死亡，回返天鄉才是靈性的出生，莊子可能是一位天上的謫仙，落入貧乏窮困的宋國來遭罪！

六、莊周喪妻、鼓盆而歌

#莊周的妻子過世了，好朋友惠施去探望他，沒料到莊子居然蹲坐在草蓆上，鼓盆而歌。這種盆是古代的一種樂器，瓦製成的罐，用小木槌輕敲，鏘然有聲。

惠施年長於莊子，用長者的口氣數落他：

「你呀，與妻子居住在一起，這麼多年來她為你生養孩子，沒有功勞也有苦勞。現在年老死了，你們感情冷淡，不哭也就罷了，居然還鼓盆而歌的慶祝，會不會太過份？」

莊子微笑的解釋：「我也沒那麼差勁，不是無情的人。起先我心裡也會難受，但又想想：生命從哪兒來的？原本無生啊！在出生之前沒有形體，當然也沒有這一股靈氣。似有若無的自然天地之間忽然變出了一股氣，這股氣凝聚成形，成形的胚胎又成為生命；如今生命又再死去。這一連串的變化完全符合春夏秋冬四季的運轉；人是大自然的一部份，如今她已安然寢息在大自然的床上，以天為被蓋、大地為臥鋪、宇宙是房間，返回天鄉，歸於原形，我何必為她嚎啕大哭呢？太看不透命理了吧！所以我才鼓盆而歌！」#

——至樂

人是大自然的一小部分，自然界四時運轉有規律，人類的生命過程也有規律，生、老、病、死，春生、夏長、秋收、冬藏，有起伏、高低潮，莊子在前章〈大宗師〉談到「化」，此章論及「變」，從虛無之中變化出微少靈氣，一點靈氣孕育出物質之形，萬物種類殊多，有的變成天上飛的、有的變作水裡游的，可能變成地上的小小螻蟻，這些小生命一旦被生出遲早總要死亡，又回復到當初無形無氣的狀態，誰能破例呢？

　　莊子沒有考慮到意志力的自我主宰性。生命變化完全依憑於不可知的天意，然而無法了解天意！這成為不可知論。安心於不可知之際的人真的滿足嗎？有些人求知慾很強，對於渺渺茫茫的天意仍然感到困惑。

七、生命多變化

　　#支離和滑介二人一塊兒遊山，到杳冥丘陵、崑崙山上黃帝休憩之地尋訪道跡。忽然之間滑介的左手肘上生出柳葉和柳枝，嚇的滑介差點驚蹶倒地！

　　　　支離看的也很訝異，問他：「你很不喜歡這樣吧？」

　　　　滑介想了想說：「也沒什麼喜歡或討厭。生命只是一種假借的現象，依附另一個軀體生出別種東西，只是塵垢罷了。生與死的關係如同晝夜，不斷交替循環，生了死、死了生，不斷生生，又不斷死生！我們二人喜歡觀察萬化，現在天地大化自動降臨在我身上，有什麼不好？我又何必心生怨憎呢？」#

———至樂

　　人的生命是一股力量的假借，別的生命寄寓在此生命上，就像草菇香蕈寄生在大樹根部，木耳寄生在潮濕的樹幹，癌細胞寄生在病患體內，跳蚤蝨子寄生在獅子、貓、犬、人體身上，櫸寄生、冬蟲夏草、海底大鯨魚都有一大批寄生的小動物，這些體積微小的寄生物不就是塵垢嗎？

　　修道人靜觀外在天地的變化，領悟天道，一旦變化降臨到自身還冷靜的起來嗎？曾傳聞有某位知名學者，一輩子講學教人修行，老年時躺在病床上，哀天喚地，脾氣暴燥，死前很不寧靜，這就是沒有真實的修為！莊子有「物化」的奇特想像，很值得回味。

八、死後的快樂

　　#莊子去南方的楚國，路上看見一具死人骨頭，他用馬鞭敲敲髑髏頭，低聲沈吟道：「先生！你是因為貧窮無棺木下葬，才暴屍於荒郊野外嗎？還是你的國家滅亡，在戰亂中被殺死而棄屍於此？或者你做了什麼羞辱門風的壞事，無顏見家人，自己尋死的？再不然你又窮又病，半路上餓死凍死的？或者你的年事已高，走不動路，倒斃在此呢？」

　　他很同情死者，撥撥土坑，將散亂的骨骸掩埋，揀起頭蓋骨，撥灰撢塵，把它當作枕頭，倚著髑髏骨安然入睡了。

　　半夜竟然夢到頭骨主人跟他說話：

　　「你今天說話的口氣倒頗像一個辯士。你所說所想的全都是一些多餘的累贅。我們死後的世界其實沒這麼多麻煩。你想不想聽我說啊？」

　　莊子很好奇，迫不及待的答：「好。」

　　髑髏主人說：「死後的生活很自由，上無君主管你，下無群臣約束你，也不必操心冬夏四時的農務工作，歲月悠悠，以天地為春秋，無倉促壓迫感，即使南面王的快樂也不過如此啦！」

　　莊子才不信呢！他追問：「如果司命真君讓你復生，令你肢體回復完好，又讓你有和樂美滿的家庭、妻子、兒女、好朋友，你難道不想要麼？」

　　髑髏主人皺起眉頭，縮著鼻子，咋舌說：「我才不要呢！我不可能放棄南面王的快樂，又去重操人世間辛酸勞苦的舊業！」#

——至樂

　　莊子的膽識夠大，見到死人骨頭不但不害怕，反而有同情心的向它詢問：怎麼死的？為何沒有人埋葬？是飢荒？是戰亂？是亡國？還是犯了罪逃亡在外？人生有窮困、衰老，這些外在因素固然逃不掉，內在因素也無法可免，人一定會死的，卻不知如何死法？中國人崇尚福、祿、壽、喜，還要子孫滿堂，壽終正寢。暴屍於荒郊野外在中國人看來是忌諱的事，「死無葬身之地」是惡毒的咀咒，卻不知西藏人的天葬要肢解屍體，讓鷲鷹來吃屍肉；大夏族人把老父丟去餵狗，印度苦行僧人自跳懸崖，把財產贈送給推他一把幫助他自殺的人。

　　出乎意料的，怎麼死法並不重要，死後快活才是重點，死後比生前快活愜意的多！生前在受罪，死後大自由！沒有君臣上下之分，沒有嚴寒酷熱之刑，沒有貧富貴賤的界域！哎！人人都快活似神仙，每個人都有南面王的得意滿足感。

死後才得到至樂。不必貪戀短暫的塵世！

九、未嘗生、未嘗死

#列子在半路上吃自己所帶的乾糧，卻見到荒煙蔓草中有枯朽的人頭髑髏，看來風化了很久，可能有百年以上。他撥開長及腰胸的蓬草，感嘆地對頭骨說：「喂！只有咱們倆個清楚：其實你既沒有死，也沒有生。死後的你真的憂愁嗎？活著的我果真快樂嗎？未必呢！」#

————至樂

生命只有一生一世嗎？

跨越了形軀，是否另有無形的永生？

列子是古代的修道人，秉持堅定的信念，了解短暫的塵世只是一系列中的一小環，如何才能明白真實生命的超越性？超越有限的時間空間，「看到」有限之後的無限。這是一道難題。到目前為止莊子以夢境覺受做譬喻，以四季循環來做類比，不知這對於一般人是否具有說服力？

十、哀莫大於心死

顏回模仿孔子，無論言行舉止、說話口氣，連走路的方式都要學！有點兒奇怪！

他問孔子：為何他學的入木三分，卻仍然遠遠不及孔子？孔子平素不言而信，不比而周，這是後生小子學不來的！孔子如此答覆：

#世界上最大的悲哀是心已死掉，其次才是形體的死亡。每天日出東方又落向西方，日日如此，從來不變，規律常存在自然界，萬物生靈都依此規律而存活，有頭手腳趾的人類也依附此種自然律來作息，每天早出晚歸，各司其職。一切生物皆如此，有所憑待的出生，有所依待的老死。我感知到身軀的物質屬性，暫時形體不會變滅，但終究要走向形化。我平日仿效萬物的生存法則，當動則動，日夜努力不息，不致偷懶怠惰，也不預期最後有什麼結果。生命原本如蒸氣雲霧一般的薰發成形，命運又不可預知，我不妄動心

念，彷彿心已死去般平靜，所以超越在你的前頭。#

　　　　　　　　　　　　　　　　　　　　　　——田子方

　　這則文章的主題應該是「有待」，萬事萬物都像日月星辰的運轉，一切有規則，靠著內在無形的天律有生有滅，有消有長；既然凡事皆其然，我們不妨息心定意，沒什麼值得掛懷，這叫做「心死」。不過修道人的「死心」無所謂悲不悲哀，心都死了，豈會悲哀？

　　莊子可能指出一個方向：要想有進境，必得死凡心；凡心若不死，不可能仿效萬物而活動。莊子認爲有先天的「命」存在，它是不可測知的。中國人的「命」有宿命、命運二詞，都指預先註定好的，當然也有人積極的想改造命運，少有人分析如何形成命運，直到印度佛教東來對此問題才有通盤性的解釋。莊子的年代佛教思想尚未萌芽，所以看的出莊子認爲人類的遭遇有不可抗拒的先天力量存在，這是素樸的天命思想，但很模糊！

十一、氣化生死

　　#生是死的延續，死是生的開始，誰說它們有固定的順序？

　　人的生命是一團氣的凝聚現象，這一股氣聚合時稱之曰生，氣消散了稱之爲死。如果生死死生是拴在一起的話，那還有什麼好耽心的！反正跑不掉，一定會發生。

　　萬物皆有生死。萬物都是氣的聚散，所以天地之間一切萬物都是相同的一個整體！你把喜愛的好東西視爲神奇傑作，把你所厭惡的視爲臭爛腐朽。其實臭爛腐朽可以變化爲神奇，神奇的東西終有一日衰朽臭腐。所以說：『整個天地萬物都是相同的一種氣罷了。』聖人很看重這種抽象的無形一致性！#

　　　　　　　　　　　　　　　　　　　　　　——知北遊

　　宋代張載的氣化論應該源自於莊子。

　　希臘哲學也認爲生命是一股氣(Pneuma)，此氣可以是呼吸，可以是靈性，也可以是生命力。反正在思想發展史上地、水、火、風、空，一共五種元素，都各有其必要性，生命現象中不可或缺。

　　不過氣化論有落入唯物思想之嫌，人的心靈豈能以僵硬的唯物主義來侷限？氣之聚散宜表達生命的不確定性，不可測知，多變化的性質上，不適宜以物化屬性來拘束精神層面。

一般人習慣說「生死」，為何不改口說：「死生」？它們之間有固定的先後秩序嗎？如果生命是一連串的鎖鏈，無始又無終，那就不能以一次生死來理解，而是多次、無數次的生生死死，死後又生，誰先誰後也不一定！

萬物各自有命！壽限長短也不同，從有限的觀點來看，萬物皆有成、住、壞、空的生命過程，有的一朝一夕，有的百年生死，參天古木千年生死，無論多麼長壽，都是有限的生命，從這一點來看確是很公平的！莊子以為一切動物、植物都是氣的聚散，所以天下萬物的生生死死只是氣的聚聚散散而已。

如果生命只是氣的聚散，不知如何解釋萬物的種類差異？難道對於生物界的繁多又要歸之於「天」嗎？這樣一切將無解，陷入惡性循環的困境。

十二、白駒過隙

#人活在天地之間，生命瞬間即逝，好像白色千里馬飛馳而過；或者像閃亮的陽光剎那間立刻消失。

年青之時如同草木欣欣向榮，雨後冒春筍一般，生機勃發；年華將逝之時，再怎麼努力也挽留不住，青春照樣如逝水流沙般消失。

生命變化成形，又歷經變化而去，自然界草木同悲，人類亦感覺哀傷！

一旦解脫生命中的桎梏，擺脫塵世的牽絆，輕鬆俐落的，魂魄要離去，身體也不堪使用了，這時才是根本的大迴歸。#

———知北遊

「白駒過隙」是很出名的常用語，《莊子》書中有的版本用「白駒過卻」，音很近似。

比較特別的是：莊子在此談到魂魄，而且與一般的思維順序顛倒，通常是：人死了，三魂七魄才離去。但莊子此處卻不同：魂魄先離去，隨後身體也離去，所以才不堪使用！這種說法也有道理，有不少老年人先失智或失去記憶，魂不守舍，拖了幾個月或幾年，生理機能才結束。有些經過車禍後意識昏迷，住院幾天後，回天乏術才死掉。

道家認為人有三魂七魄，莊子只說「魂魄」，至少他同意氣化成形後人類有魂魄，但魂魄是不是「氣」呢？哪一團氣包括了肉體和精神？魂魄與氣一定有關，氣包含生理與心理二種成份，能否再辨認氣中哪一部份化爲魂魄？哪一部份凝聚成爲身軀？氣如何分清濁、陰陽？這是後世宋明理學想要處理的難題。

十三、死生一體

#不必以「生命」推動死亡，

　　也不必以「死亡」結束生命。

　　死與生是彼此相互依靠的嗎？

　　它們合起來成爲一個整體？

　　還是各自爲一體？

　　或者源自於一個大來源？#

　　　　　　　　　　　　　　　　　　　　　　　　────

　　通常人視「生」之後有結束，有生必有死。死亡是生命的終點。但莊子有意改變這種思維方式，「死亡」未必是從「生」產生，「死亡」未必結束生命，說不定它自身比「生」更有意義，更有價值。有積極價值的東西值得我們期待，如此「死亡」不是生命的尾端，而是另一段新生命的開始！

　　莊子沒有用肯定語氣來認定死亡的積極性，只是以反向思考的疑問句來激發思維，他的用意在突破傳統成見，不預設答案，只給予一個新方向，讓你自己思考下去。

　　死與生的關係是否相對待？有此必有彼，生與死都繫縛在生命本體上，一頭一尾，它們應當屬於一個整體；既然在一個主體上，也就無所謂是否爲相對待了。

十四、三種生死觀

　　莊子綜合整理前面所提出的人生態度，對它們作出高低評價：

　　#上古時候的人知識程度有限，對於生命的看法有所不同：

　　　　第一種人，以爲世界上根本無物存在，「本來無一物」，於此觀念下一切隨緣放曠，這就是至善至美的境域了。宇宙洪荒之時，原本一切尚未成形，混沌一片，既無生命，也無死亡，天地未分之際本來無一物，所以不必再談什麼生生死死。

第二種人，以為宇宙自然界是一個整體，一個浩大的存有物，也是生命的根源；萬物生靈從此根源分化而出，將來亦回歸於此。從天地的本位來看，分化出去的生命喪失了母源頭，必須等死後才能返回天鄉。這種由天地源流分化出生命，又返回歸一的過程與上述「混沌無一物」的思想已經逕渭分明了。

第三種思想更是精密，起先無一物存在，後來發生了生命現象，生之後有死；或者主張：一切生靈以空無為頭，以生命為軀體，以死亡為尾椎；誰能看破生死關，了解生、死、有、無，本為一體，才夠資格相與論道。#

———庚桑楚

莊子認為：表面上這三種想法有精粗之分，其實骨子裡完全一樣，就像人的姓氏，有人因官位而有姓氏、有的人因封地而有姓氏，其實這些都是虛名，重要的是內容都一樣，反正生與死是一個整體，分不開的。你若接受了生命的美好，也得接受死亡的安息。不必心懷恐懼。

十五、感傷

#莊子為一位朋友送葬，正好經過惠施的墳墓，此情此景，想起往事，對旁邊隨行的弟子們說：

「春秋時楚國有位江陵人士，特意在鼻尖上沾了一小點白堊土，細薄如蒼蠅翅膀，叫他的好朋友石匠揮動斧頭去掉。他不怕鼻子被切割掉。石匠也蠻不在乎的舞動斧頭，技巧熟練的去掉白堊土而不傷及鼻尖。江陵人站著，面色如常，也不害怕，對石匠朋友很有信心。這椿事被宋元君知道了，感到好奇又好玩。叫這位石匠來，也為宋元君去除鼻尖小白堊土，作個現場表演。石匠拒絕君王，理由是：『過去我確實辦得到，這全靠對方的配合。如今這位對手已過世，我也不願再找其他人做實驗。』

莊子黯然的說：「自從惠施夫子過世後，我也失去了一個對手。沒人跟我辯論聊天了。」#

———徐無鬼

看來莊子表面上灑脫、看得開、放得下，其實還是很有感情，他的生死觀一再強調死亡是解脫累贅懸疣，死亡是返歸天鄉，死後很快樂！勝過當南面王……。但畢竟懷念昔日的相談之歡，這也令人感嘆失去好朋友的落寞。朋友可以再交新的，但知交摯友卻難得一二人。直爽的莊子一向語出驚人又不吐不快，如今無人可共談，辯論要看對手！智力反應要相當，默契交心妙不可言，如今這些都難再尋了。死亡雖與生命為一體，但其間過程的酸、甜、苦辣還是很刻骨銘心的。

十六、到底有沒有鬼？

#世人大多做有為之事，早晚邁向死亡之途，像這樣的死是有緣由的；反觀萬物草木，無心自發，欣欣向榮，無所為而存活，是沒什麼緣由的。

　　人與物果然如此嗎？怎麼樣才是適當之舉？怎麼樣是不當的行徑？天有天理，人有人道。自然界有四季循環，江山大地有地域分隔，我要尋求什麼呢？我能知道多少呢？對於自然萬物無法確定它的終點，怎麼會走盡生命呢？對於萬物無法得知它的源頭，它怎麼發生了呢？

　　有些人稟賦有異精神上有微妙感應，認為世上有鬼。也有人一輩子渾然不覺，不能與幽冥界相應，對這些人如何證明有鬼呢？#

———寓言

　　此篇文章透入形上學的幽思，講到天地之起始，生命的發生，不但有陽世而且有陰間；有些人能感應，有些人感應不到。

　　莊子未細談與鬼相應的內容，他是相當理性的懷疑論者，用客觀的雙向思考做兩端扣擊，沒有固定答案，只是敲響二方論題，讓後人自己去思考。

　　有感應的未必是鬼，天地間除了人、鬼、動物之外還有其他，這屬於宗教的範圍了。

十七、莊子臨終

#莊子年老，臨終之前弟子們私下商量：要給夫子辦個風光又隆重的喪禮。躺在床上的莊子耳朵還很靈光，聽到他們的計劃，叫弟子們過來吩咐：

　　「一向我很看的開，死後就以天地為棺槨，以燦爛光輝的日月為腰帶玉佩連璧，以天上亮晶晶的星辰為帽沿珠璣。自然界所有的草木動物都為我送行，我的葬禮豈不已很完備？何必勞師動眾又破費呢？」

　　弟子滿心憐憫的說：「我們擔心夫子的身體在荒郊野外被烏鴉老鷹給

啄食了。」

　　莊子微微笑說：「哎！天上有烏鴉老鷹來吃我的屍體，地下也有螞蟻昆蟲來蛀食我的屍體，這有什麼差別？何必奪此又與彼，豈不偏心哪？」#

——列禦寇

莊子臨死還愛開玩笑，不在乎自己的身體被誰吃掉。有夫妻二人吵架，婦人發潑，尋死尋活，丈夫冷言冷語：「你去尋死吧！我才懶得給你買棺材，丟給你一張草蓆就不錯了！」

婦人為了這句話懷恨丈夫數十年，始終怨恨丈夫刻薄。

莊子灑脫的情懷如清風明月，胸襟如此開闊！臨死前毫不掛心他的喪事，的確不是俗人。莊子壽終正寢，死得其所，在戰國時代可真是一種福分！

結語

莊子為自己的生死觀作了三種區分：

第一種：大自然原本混沌一片，宇宙天地無始無終，倒溯回無時間、無空間的本然狀態，本來無生也無死，一切萬有尚未成形，生命之初的源頭無以名之，本來無一物，何必談論生生死死？

這種渾沌本源的回歸狀態是形上學中的宇宙論，跳脫了人世間的所有歷程，不理會生理、心理、精神的波浪起伏，很超脫，但也很遙遠！

第二種：人來自於大自然的造化，造物者有祂造化的本意，被造者不能參與意見，不能挑三選四的說：「我要當一把名劍。」或說：「我要當一個有錢人。」人被造物者造出生命，當然也安排了死亡。死亡正好是返回天鄉，與造物者合一。造物者已經為我們安排好生命過程：大地承載著身軀，提供日常生活所需，工作是疲累的，老年時卸下重擔，得以閒暇休息；時候到了就該完全放棄生命，接受死亡的解脫，在此期間放棄自主意識是一項訴求，一切隨順先天命運的安排，絲毫沒有反抗天意的意志力。於此「無我」的訴求來看，莊子繼承了老子「柔弱」的個性，對於天意，大自然、命運、絲毫不加以反抗，完全順隨天意，這可稱之為「柔弱哲學」，也是老子「上善若水」的體悟表現。

　　第三種思想比第一種具體，比第二種完備，認為：以空無為頭首，以生命發展為脊椎，以死亡為尾椎；置生死於度外，無始無終，無出無入，生生死死是分不開的一個整體，唯有安然接受死亡，才能完成一個生命整體！

　　莊子認為本質上這三種想法都一樣，反正視生死為不可分離的「一」，小一與造化相結合為更大的「一」，當然結合有結合的步驟，這就是莊子的修養工夫論了！

　　不可諱言的，莊子的修養工夫影響後世道家相當深遠，它有系統、有步驟，是禪法的一種，但在研究莊禪之前還有一項課題也應該明白掌握，那就是他的人生哲學。

　　莊子的人生觀堪稱複雜，有時重視形體外貌，說生靈由氣化而來，「氣化論」在後代有誤入唯物主義的危險；有時他又談神說鬼，顯然走向神秘主義；再有時崇尚至人、真人、聖人、神人，有超人主義的虛玄味道，不食人間煙火，清虛寡慾、逃名棄利、修出世法。他經常談命運、面相術，更多提到性與心的問題，龐雜的很。他的道德觀又不同於儒家的道德觀，所以理解他的人生哲學甚不容易。

　　平常莊子談神人、真人、至人，臨終前不談這些，反而笑談以天地為棺槨、以落葉為被蓋；上有蒼鷹啄食，下有螻蟻蛀食。他的境界既虛玄超越，又平易實在，生死與死生沒二樣，在他看來：死亡是另一個生命，一個值得重視的超越階段。

參考書目：

*1.*莊子原典，陳鼓應註，莊子今註今譯，台北，商務印書館，80 年，十版。

*2.*玄默編著，莊子的智慧，台北，國家出版社，77 年。

*3.*錢穆著，莊子纂箋，香港，東南印務出版社，1963。

*4.*張默生著，莊子新釋，台灣、綠州書局。

*5.*陳鼓應主編：莊子與兩晉佛學般若思想，文史哲出版社，89 年。

The Ultimate Quest: Saul Bellow's *Ravelstein*

林莉莉
Li-li Lin
國防醫學院
人文及社會科學科
副教授

摘　　要

Ravelstein 集合索爾貝婁過去的重要主題，並藉由哲學家的死亡宣告一個時代的結束。本文試圖證明，八十七高齡的貝婁仍不放棄藉由小說召告世人，藝術和愛才是人類最終的救贖。

After the publication of *The Theft* in 1989, Saul Bellow claimed that the novella form gave him "great pleasure to be more concise and quick." And he would be publishing another novella *The Bellarosa Connection* in the same year. He said, "Maybe it's my age, . . . Maybe I think I have a great many unfinished things to do, and that I know I can do these novellas handily" (Coughlin 6E). Eleven years later, in 2000, when he was 85, the Nobel laureate published a novel of 230 pages, though not as long as his previous novels, he did surprised the reader. Besides, he also returned to his old subject, intellectuals; this time, a straight academic figure, though a gay, a world-famous heavyweight political science professor. All subjects Bellow has long been exploring are incorporated into this novel. At age 85, Saul Bellow is still asking, "What is it that makes us all human?" (Weinstein, "*Dean's*" 31). His Jewish characters are still haunted, and even more frequently, by the Holocaust (Kremer 15) after he makes them "stereotypes" of the victim in *The Victim* (Wirth-Nesher & Malamut 60). They are still taking journeys for their life-long quest of identity and love.

Abe Ravelstein is a very popular political science professor teaching at a university in Chicago. His friend Chick, a prize-winning writer, suggests him to publish his classroom notes. Though Ravelstein never prepares them, he publishes a book about his ideas and becomes world-famous and a millionaire. He then asks Chick to write a book about him. Soon after that, Ravelstein dies of AIDS. Six years after he dies, Chick experiences near-death during a trip to the Caribbean with his wife Rosamund. He decides to put his words into action—to write a book in memory of Abe Ravelstein.

Is this memoir just about Ravelstein? It is initiated by a short account of J. M. Keynes, a famous economist-statesman, whom Ravelstein has encouraged Chick to write about. In a conversation, Ravelstein says to Chick, "I want you to do me as you did Keynes, but on a bigger scale. And also you were too kind to him. I don't want that. Be as hard on me as you like . . . by describing me maybe you'll emancipate yourself" from, in Chick's words, "Dimwitoclese" (13)*. Is Chick released from the so-called "Dimwitoclese"? In some way, yes. After experiencing near-death and believing love of his wife has brought him back to life, he thinks of Ravelstein: "I don't suppose when he directed me to write an account of his life he expected me to settle for what was characteristic — characteristic of me, is what I mean, naturally" (186). This near-death experience also enhances the sense of transience of life in Chick. He says, "Our way of organizing the data which rush by in gestalt style--that is, in increasingly abstract forms--speeds up experiences into a dangerously topsy-turvy fast-forward comedy. Our need for rapid disposal eliminates the details that bewitch, hold, or delay the children. Art is one rescuer from this chaotic acceleration. . . . But we do feel that we are speeding earthward, crashing into our graves." He says to his wife, "But I feel it every day. Powerless thinking itself eats up what is left of life. . . "(192). He has talked to Ravelstein about this, but his own dying experience pushes him to grasp the dead with art--that is, writing the memoir. In addition to this, Chick believes that the dead "are not gone for good" (187). By writing a memoir he can stop the chariot of time from running and bring back the dead. In the last one and a half pages of this novel, Ravelstein has returned to life and Chick describes the situation in simple present tense. *Ravelstein* serves as Bellow's belief in art.

In his old age Bellow still concerns about art. Ravelstein's best-seller that makes him a millionaire criticizes liberal education in the United States. He argues that "while you could get an excellent technical training in the U.S., liberal education had shrunk to the vanishing point. . . . No real education was possible in American universities except for aeronautical engineers, computerists, and the like. The universities were excellent in biology and physical sciences, but the liberal arts were a failure. . . . philosophy was finished. . . ." (47). Chick also complains that people do not read literary classics any more. He says, "In the old days there was still a considerable literary community in our country, and medicine and law were still 'the learned professions,' but in an American city today you can no longer count on doctors, lawyers, businessmen, journalists, politicians, television personalities, architects, or commodities traders to discuss Stendhal's novels or Thomas Hardy's poems" (46). In an interview with Joseph Epstein, Bellow talks about "the rather demoralizing effect of literature in our universities" (In Cronin & Siegel 134). And in a self-interview, he says, "The teaching of literature has been a disaster" (Bellow, In Cronin & Siegel 116). In the same interview when talking about literary culture in Paris, Bellow says, "What is certain is that we have nothing like it in America--no Maitres except in dining rooms, no literary world, no literary public. Many of us read, many love literature, but the traditions and institutions of literary culture are lacking" (113). Chick is speaking for Saul bellow in this novel.

There is one more indispensable reason for Chick to write the memoir. Before Ravelstein dies he says to Chick many times, "You could do a really fine memoir. It's not just a request, . . . I'm laying this on you as an obligation" (129). Chick tells the reader, "In choosing me or setting me up to write this memoir, he obliged me to consider my death as well as his. And not only his death from shingles . . . but a good many other deaths as well. It was collection time for an entire generation" (129-30). In other words, this novel is a memoir of one generation, an elegy for the death of one generation, instead of one person.

There are two physical trips, Ravelstein and Chick's trip to Paris and Chick and Rosamund's trip to the Caribbean, and Chick's mental trip in writing the memoir. The trip to Paris builds Ravelstein up as a Bellovian Everyman, the representative of one generation of the intellectual, and a typical Jewish intellectual who is obsessed with the Holocaust and is talking about love or Eros all the time. And the trip to the Caribbean is a sort of a trip between life and death to Chick. It makes Chick confirms again the power of love that can bring a man back to life, both his and Ravelstein's. It also reminds him that life is short and art is "one rescue" and a major one.

Ravelstein is a "large man" with "a tremendous eager energy" (3). He never gets rest, even when he is lying dead (66). The "whiteness" of his big bald head is somewhat "dangerous" (19). His feet are "mismatched." "One was three sizes bigger than the other" (18). He always begins "every clause in his long sentences with 'Thee-ah, thee-ah, thee-ah'" (18). He is sort of a father to his students. Once "they became his intimates he planned their futures." "He gave much thought to student matches" (27). Chick gives him epitaphs like "Ravelstein the Jewish comedian" (23), and "Ravelstein the sinner" (31). Referring to Ravelstein's large size, Chick says he "could wear clothes with more dramatic effect . . . A tragic hero has to be above the average in height" (30). Once when they are talking about death Chick says, Ravelstein's "serious preoccupations 'coexisted' . . . with his buffoonery" (44). Ravelstein also says that he can play the "buffoon" when teaching Platonic dialogues (45). Ravelstein is also an atheist who does not believe in life after death. Ravelstein loves scandals and gossips a lot. People call from Paris, London, and Washington to keep him informed, therefore he is always talking on the phone. Chick writes, "I said he must be masterminding a shadow government. He accepted this, smiling as though the oddity were not his but mine" (12).Further more, Ravelstein holds basketball parties for graduate students, even after he is sick. While they are watching games on TV in his living room, they "found in these entertainment a common ground between the fan clubs of childhood and the Promised Land of the intellect toward which Ravelstein, their Moses and their Socrates, led them.

Michael Jordan was now an American cult figure . . . Inevitably Ravelstein was seen by the young men he was training as the intellectual counterpart to Jordan" (57). Once when Ravelstein and Chick are talking about sex, Ravelstein says that Chick is "an anachronism." Chick's comment on Ravelstein is: "Mixtures of arch-aism and modernity were especially appealing to Ravelstein, who could not be con-tained in modernity and overflowed all the ages. Oddly enough, he was just like that" (69). All these characteristics being merged in one person indicates that Rav-elstein is deliberately molded as an Everyman. Since Ravelstein is suffering from AIDS, the Plague of the Twentieth-century, he is also an embodiment of a universal victim.

When discussing about *Mr. Sammler's Planet*, Wirth-Nesher & Malamut point out, Bellow's "success rests mainly on his ability to undermine the expectations re-aders have developed about Jewish subjects like the Holocaust or the State of Israel" (59). Holocaust is mentioned a few times, and Ravelstein reminds Chick that Chick's ex-wife Vela's friend Radu Grielescu is once a follower of Nae Ionesco, the founder of the Iron Guard. But to Chick Grielescu seems to be a gentle and erudite man, who seldom talks about politics but about archaic history or mythology (127). Nazi followers and fascists have become normal people. Though Ravelstein talks about them, he doesn't even really care about people who are killed in the Gulags or fascists concentration camps. He cares more about the nihilism that pervades Europe. Chick explains, "But the maddest forms of nihilism are the most strict Ger-man military ones. . . . For the rank-and-file this led to the bloodies and craziest kind of revanchist murderous zeal. Because it was implicit in carrying out orders. And everybody was thus absolved. They were crazies through and through. And this was the Wehrmacht way of getting around responsibility for their crimes" (168). Chick days to his wife, " . . . there was a general willingness to live with the destruction of millions. It was the mood of the century to accept it. . . . Why does the century--I don't know how else to put it--underwrite so much destruction? There is a lameness that comes over all of us when we consider these facts" (169). What Ravelstein, and also Chick, care about is the nihilism and people's indifference to the Holocaust.

While Ravelstein is described as an Everyman who is suffering from the Plague of the Century, AIDS is compared to the Holocaust. While the novel is a memoir of an entire generation, Ravelstein's death can be compared to the death of an entire generation. While Nazi has been the executioner of the Jew, AIDS can be the executioner of genocide. While what is horrifying is nihilism and indifference, the only solution to this centurial problem is love.

Ravelstein is characterized as a political science professor who always talks about love and believes in love. Chick says that Ravelstein "rated longing very highly. Looking for love, falling in love, you were pining for the other half you had lost, as Aristophanes had said" (24). Based on the myth, men and women "defied the Olympian Gods who punished them by splitting them in half. This is the mutilation that mankind suffered. So that generation after generation we seek the missing half, longing to be whole again" (24). This belief is very important to Ravelstein. Chick says, "If you didn't know this about him, you couldn't know him at all. Without its longings your soul was a used inner tube maybe good for one summer at the beach, nothing more. Spirited men and women, the young above all, were devoted to the pursuit of love. . . . There, in the briefest form possible, you have a sketch of Ravelstein's most important preoccupations" (25). The Greek word Eros is mentioned several times. "With the help of Eros we go on, each of us, looking for his missing half" (82). According to Ravelstein, "We have to keep life going, one way or another. Marriage must be made. . . . But for most of mankind the longings have, one way or another, been eliminated (italics mine)" (83). This love between man and woman is, for Bellow, a final resort for human beings. In a novella, *The Actual* (1997), Harry Trellman's quest for self-identity is completed by returning to his home town and marrying his high school sweetheart (Lin, "Harry Trellman").

Chick and Rosamund's trip to the Caribbean also makes Chick realize the power of love from his wife. Her love brings him back to life from a disease which has never been identifies. When thinking of writing a memoir of Ravelstein after recovering from the illness, Chick says, "I am a great believer in the power of unfinished work to keep you alive. But your survival can't be explained by this simple one-to-one abstract equivalence. Rosamund kept me from dying" (231). Love and the unfinished business keep Chick alive. As I have referred to, in my "Harry Trellman's Quest for Self-identity," I would like to do it again, in an interview with Susan Crosland, Bellow talks about "'the ordeal of desire' that is starving the western world. Women, as well as men, invite the death of love by the literalness of their imagination" (In Cronin & Siegel 235). Bellow still believes in love.

As one of Ravelstein's favorite students, Rosamund also believes in love. She tells Chick when Ravelstein talks about Ivan Ilyich's marriage, he says, " . . .that if he and his wife had loved each other things would have looked different." "The poor things did hate each other," says Rosamund. "Reading that story is like crossing a mountain of broken glass. It's an ordeal" (192). Ravelstein also refers to Chick's twelve-year's marriage to his ex-wife Vela, who files for divorce soon after Chick has buried his two brothers, as "a prison term you (Chick) sentenced yourself to" (112). Where there is no love, there is no redemption. Again, love between man and woman is celebrated in this novel. We may say that it is Bellow's ultimate goal in his life long quest.

Ravelstein and Chick have different views about death. Ravelstein is an atheist, while Chick believes there is life after death. He tells his wife, "If I were to write my memoir of Ravelstein there would be no barrier between death and me" (163). But we know before he writes it, he "went through a rehearsal" of his own death (161). After Ravelstein dies, Chick and his wife talk about him "almost daily" but, he says, " I couldn't for the life of me find this starting point." Rosamund tells him, "All you need is to get yourself in the right position" (162). The "right position" turns out to be a near-death experience. That is how he gets connections with the dead.

When it comes to terms with the dead, academic training is not available. Preparing to write a book about Ravelstein, Chick has already studied five or six books written by Whitehead and Russell. Ravelstein "sharply" tells him not to do that. Even though he is trying to write about a political philosopher, he doesn't need to read about other philosophers. Just like Rosamund has studied love—"Rousseauan romantic love and the Platonic Eros as well, with Ravelstein—but she knew far more about it than either her teacher or her husband" from real life. What Chick needs is to connect with the dead in person. He says, "But I would rather see Ravelstein again than to explain matters it doesn't help to explain" (231). The last part of the memoir is written in simple present tense. In Chick's delusion, or a motion picture produced by his memory, Ravelstein is on the scene just as he used to be. When he is disappearing, he "loses himself in sublime music, a music in which ideas are dissolved, reflecting these ideas in the form of feeling. He carries them down into the street with him. There's an early snow on the tall shrubs, the same shrubs filled with a huge flock of parrots—the ones that escaped from cages and now build their long nest sacks in the back alleys . . . Ravelstein looks at me, laughing with pleasure and astonishment, gesturing because he can't be heard in all this bird-noise" (232-33). The unfinished business comprises both his promise and love to Ravelstein. Ravelstein doesn't want Chick to write about his ideas; only when they are reflected "in the form of feeling" can they bring Chick to work. Ravelstein has been a "voracious eater," but before he dies, his "meals were now mainly social, conversational occasions" (142). He just talks before he dies. But in Chick's delusion he stops talking for the parrots.

The parrots appear three times in the novel. The first time Ravelstein sees them, he is indifferent to them because nature does not appeal to him. He likes people and big cities; country bores him. The second time he sees them when he is discharged from hospital after a fatal attack of the disease. And he is surprised that he is delighted to see the parrots. In this sense, the parrots symbolizes life and re-birth to him. The snow is a conventional symbol of death. When Ravelstein is walking into the snow he sees the flock of parrots. It signifies that he will be given life again in the memoir written by Chick.

This novel again proves that Saul Bellow believes in the power of art and love and they can connect the past and the present and bring human into future.

*Hereafter quotations from *Ravelstein* will be given page numbers only.

Works Cited

Bellow Saul. "Some Questions and Answers." In Cronin & Siegel. 113-121.

Bellow, Saul. *Ravelstein*. New York: Penguin Putnam, 2000.

Coughlin, Ruth Rollack. "Mellow Bellow." *The Detroit News* (Tuesday, 18 April 1989): 1E, 6E.

Cronin, Gloria L. and Ben Siegel, eds. *Conversations with Saul Bellow*. Jackson: UP of Mississippi, 1994.

Crosland, Susan. "Bellow's Real Gift." In Cronin & Siegel. 230-35.

Epstein, Joseph. "A Talk with Saul Bellow." In Cronin & Siegel. 132-139.

Kremer, S. Lillian. "The Holocaust in *The Victim*." *Saul Bellow Journal*, 2; ii (Spring-Summer 1983): 15-23.

Lin, Li-li. "Harry Trellman's Quest for Self-identity." *Yuan-Yuan Yearly* 12 (Taipei, November 24, 2000):125-30.

Weinstein, Ann. "*The Dean's December*: Bellow's Plea for the Humanities and Humanity." *Saul Bellow Journal* 2.2 (Spring-Summer 1983): 30-41.

Wirth-Nesher, Hana & Andrea Cohen Malamut. "Jewish And Human Survival On Bellow's Planet." *Modern Fiction Studies* 25: 59-74.

Survival in *Crossing the River*

康家麗

Chia-Li Kang

國防醫學院

人文及社會科學科副教授

摘　　要

　　流離失所，顛沛困頓是二百五十年來散落世界各地非裔奴隸及其子孫之集體記憶。本文旨在探討非裔黑人奴隸及其後代如何憑藉其強烈之求生意志，過人之耐力及毅力，克服生命中的困厄，而終得以倖存之過程。

In Gayl Jones' *Corregidora*, the memories of slavery and the hatred of Corregidora are passed through the generations, told and retold in order not to be forgotten while the stories in Toni Morrison's *Beloved* have to be told because they can't be forgotten. In Sherley Anne Williams' *Dessa Rose*, stories about slavery not only have to be told, but they have to be told from Dessa's perspective and in her own voice. Through challenging Nehemiah's authority to define her in the dominant discourse and seizing discursive control of the story, Dessa rejects white, male attempts to write and read black female subjectivity—"My mind wanders. This is why I have it down, why I has the child say it back. I never will forget Nemi trying to read (and write) me, knowing I had put myself in his hands. Well, this the childrens have heard from our own lips" (In *Dessa Rose* 236).

Collective memory is not new to Caryl Phillips' *Crossing the River*. However, in *Crossing the River*, collective memory, called "the chorus of common memory" (1)*, is not just a recognition of one particular story of slavery, but an encompassing of the histories of all Africans in the Diaspora from the moment of enslavement through their struggles of today. Phillips accomplishes this by recounting the stories of three siblings sold into slavery by their father who "soiled (his) hands with cold goods in exchange for (his children's) warm flesh" because "The crops failed" (1). Each sibling is represented in a different time, establishing a bond between those in the Diaspora. Structured in four parts, the novel is set in different sites and historical moments, from nineteenth-century Africa to the United States in the years surrounding the Civil War, to the Middle Passage from 1752 to 1753, and finally to "somewhere in England" from 1936 to 1963.

History has always been a main concern for writers in the Diaspora. Asked why a great number of Afro-American novelists turn to history, Toni Morrison replies:

> It's got to be because we are responsible. I am very gratified by the fact that black writers are learning to grow in that area. We have abandoned a lot of valuable material. We live in a land where the past is always erased and America is the innocent future in which immigrants can come and start over, where the slate is clean. The past is absent or it's romanticized. This culture doesn't encourage dwelling on, let alone coming to terms with, the truth about the past. That memory is much more in danger now than it was thirty years ago. (In Paul Gilroy 179)

Black writers have turned to the past because they want to be responsible and through learning from "a lot of valuable material," they can understand where they come from, who they are and where they are going. The reassessment of the past is, in Benedicte Ledent's words, "a source of regeneration and identity for the rootless and dismembered peoples of former colonies" (In "Remembering Slavery" 271). History has to be preserved because it is crucial to survival.

Caryl Phillips dedicated his novel to "those who crossed the river." Listening to their neglected if not forgotten voices, he has created a "dialogic, interconnected narrative" (In Johanna Garvey 260) of people whom the narrator calls "my children" (1). Identifying the peculiar form which Phillips uses in *Crossing the River* to reposition the black diasporic experience in relation to conventional historical narrative form, Anthony Ilona praises the authorial attempt to present a voice that "had never before been recorded on such an epic scale" (In Anthony Ilona 3). In a novel that addresses the African diasporic experience spanning a period of 250 years, the writer is trying to establish a bond between those in the Diaspora, and furthermore, he is demonstrating the continuing necessity of the novel's message: this "chorus" is intended not only to preserve history, but to inspire the ultimate goal of survival.

Commenting on the ending of the novel, Phillips remarks:

> I perceive an annealing force that comes out of fracture. . . . I have seen some connectedness and 'celebrated' the qualities of survival that people in all sorts of predicaments are able to keep hold of with clenched fists. I didn't want to leave this novel as an analysis of fracture, because I felt such an overwhelming, passionate attachment to all the vices, and I kept thinking it seemed almost choral. These people were talking in harmonies I could hear. (Quoted in Benedicte Ledent's "Overlapping Territories" 59)

The novel opens with an African father who remembers that, 250 years before, he sold his three children, two sons and one daughter, to an British slave trader. Ever since this "shameful intercourse" (1), the guilt-ridden father has been haunted by the "chorus of a common memory" (1):

> For two hundred and fifty years I have listened to the many-tongued chorus. And occasionally, among the sundry restless voices, I have discovered those of my own children. My Nash. My Martha. My Travis. Their lives fractured. Sinking hopeful roots into difficult soil. For two hundred and fifty years I have longed to tell them: Children, I am your father, I love you. But understand. There are no paths in water. No signposts. There is no return. . . . You are beyond. Broken-off, like limbs from a tree. But not lost, for you carry within your bodies the seeds of new trees. (pp. 1-2)

Each chapter in the novel tells the story of survival. It is an interesting paradox considering that in all except "Crossing the River," the story ends in death for the protagonist. But each, in his or her own way, has survived. In the first story, Nash, a former slave of Edward Williams, operates as a black American missionary in Liberia in the 1830s under Edward's patronage. However, he disappears soon and Edward decides to go to Liberia in search of his beloved protege. In the meanwhile, Nash's unreceived letters to Edward show that he gradually becomes assimilated into African life. Though not able to completely assimilate on his mission to Africa, Nash renounces the teachings of his former white master and adapts to the ways of the natives. In his last letter he writes "this Commonwealth of Liberia has provided me with the opportunity to open up my eyes and cast off the garb of ignorance which has encompassed me all too securely the whole course of my life"(61-62). Nash knows that he will never return to America and thus "freely choose to live the life of the African"(62). He dies a free man. Survival is accomplished here through adaptation.

In the second part titled "West," the story opens with an aging Martha freezing to near death in Colorado. In her hallucination, she is reunited with her daughter Eliza Mae who was taken away in her early childhood by slave auctioneers. For Martha, survival is in her hopes—her thoughts of meeting her daughter again spur her on, enabling her to escape slavery and later attempt the journey to California. While she does not survive the pioneering journey, Martha lives to an old age.

The third section of the novel "Crossing the River" is devoted to James Hamilton, the English captain who bought the three children in 1753. In the form of a journal, Captain Hamilton records the repetitious exchange of goods for people and the increasing illness and deaths of the slaves off the Seirra Leone coast. To quote his journal entry for Monday 16th of November 1753:

> . . . Put a fresh cargo into the yawl. Left the ship before noon and rowed into shore. Was shown 11 slaves, of whom I picked 5, viz., 4 men, 1 woman. Paid what goods I had in the boat were suitable and I am to send the rest . . . (105)

Africans become a list of numbers, categorized by age, sex, physical condition and price. After dealing with illness, deaths and threats of insurrection of the slaves, Hamilton finally finishes his mission to purchase 210 slaves and prepares to leave the coast. The vessel is loaded with slaves who "huddle together, and sing their melancholy lamentations" (124). From the moment of departure, the African people have lost sight of their homeland and gone on a journey promising no reverse passage. In a fictional recreation of the events in the slave trade, Phillips depicts the great loss that marks all experience of the African diaspora.

Although "Crossing the River" may parallel actual documents of slavers, the story is the one that sets all the other three into motion and it is this story that invokes the common memory. Perhaps there is "no paths in water. No signposts" and "no return" (237), somehow some of the slaves survive. The survival of the slaves in "Crossing the River" allows the other stories to be told. Many slaves did not survive the Middle Passage, and those who did were strong and used their intelligence to find ways to live. The message for the slaves becomes the message for a people with voices "hurt but determined, they will survive the hardships of the far bank" (235).

The final part entitled "Somewhere in England" tells the tale of Travis, an American GI stationed in Britain during the Second World War. Travis is persecuted by the white-controlled army even though he is fighting for his country. Travis, however, falls in love with Joyce, a Yorkshire woman during the breakdown of her marriage to an alcoholic and abusive husband. Getting pregnant, she is alienated from the others in her town for coupling with a black man and forbidden to go to the US as Travis' wife by the Jim Crow segregation laws. Ultimately, though, Travis dies in the war. Yet, even here, survival continues, through a son, Greer, who is given up to the County Council as an orphan and returns in 1963 to visit Joyce. Greer is the only survivor of the novel; he becomes the hope for the future.

Crossing the River is mainly about survival. Survival is accomplished in many ways: through adaptation, through hope, through procreation, through strength and endurance. The will to survive is found not just in the stories of the past, but in the faces of the Diaspora today: "a helplessly addicted mother wait(ing) for the mist to clear from her eyes" in Brooklyn, "A barefoot boy"(235) who attempts to farm his barren land in Sao Paulo, an eleven-year-old premature prostitute in Santo Domingo. These are the people whom the anonymous father in the novel calls "Survivors" (236). The survival of the many, the unnamed father claims, can be heard every-where—"a many-tongued chorus continues to swell" (237). Many Africans may have been taken away from their homeland by force or by trade, but they have "arrived on the far bank of the river, loved" (237).

　　*Hereafter quotations from Caryl Phillips' *Crossing the River* will be given page numbers only.

Works Cited

Garvey, Johanna X. K. "Passages to Identity: Re-Membering the Diaspora in Marshall, Phillips, and Cliff." *Black Imagination and the Middle Passage*. Eds. Maria Diedrich, Henry Louis Gates, Jr. and Carl Pedersen. New York: Oxford UP, 1999. 255-70.

Gilroy, Paul. *Small Acts*. London: Serpent's Tail, 1993.

Ilona, Anthony. "*Crossing the River*: A Chronicle of the Black Diaspora." *Wasafiri* 22 (Autumn 1995): 3-9.

Jones, Gayl. *Corregidora*. Boston: Beacon Press, 1975.

Ledent, Benedicte. "Overlapping Territories, Interwined Histories: Cross-Culturality in Caryl Phillips's *Crossing the River.*" *Journal of Commonwealth Literature* 30:1 (1995): 55-62.

————, "Remembering Slavery: History as Roots in the Fiction of Caryl Phillips and Fred D'Aguiar." *The Contact and the Culmination*. Eds. Marc Delrez and Benedicte Ledent. Liege, Belgium: L, Liege Language and Literature, 1997. 271-80.

Morrison, Toni. *Beloved*. New York: Knopf. 1987.

Phillips, Caryl. *Crossing the River*. New York: Vintage International, 1995.

Williams, Sherley Anne. *Dessa Rose*. New York: William Morrow, 1986.

Mary Tyrone's Quest for the Past

王丹青
Dan-ching Wang
國防醫學院
人文及社會科學科講師

摘　　要

　　對於現實生活的不滿，Mary Tyrone 選擇：逃避，退縮到少女求學時代，卻不願面對現實。為了排遣孤獨、消除痛苦，她沉迷於吸食嗎啡，而得了精神錯亂症。一味追尋過去的結果，除了她自己跌進更深的過去，無法逃脫之外，也將她的家人推入痛苦的深淵。

In *Long Day's Journey into Night*, for all the four Tyrones, it is a journey into the past. But for Mary, mother of the family, it is much longer and bitter on the day in August, 1912. She only dreams of the past. As the play moves on, she is trying to escape the pain of the present. Her unhappy memories not only make herself suffer but the whole family as well. In so doing, she gives a decisively situational change during this long day's journey because she does not give up drug addiction for the sake of enjoying her girlhood after staying two months in the sanatorium. It releases unexpected reactions from her husband, James, a famous actor, her first son, Jamie, an actor too, but a failure and an alcoholic, and the younger son, a journalist who is going to be sent to a tuberculosis hospital. Under the influence of morphine, all B males of the Tyrone family, pursue oblivion in alcohol for the sake of removing the pain occupying their mind. Time in the play "evaporates and hovers, and disappears: past, present, future become one" (Brustein, in Bloom 28). Time as an adjunct of the present has stopped; forward motion has ended. The slow turning of memory is the play's main action. Mary Tyrone's quest "represents each person's search for the meaning of one's life, of which only memory has the secret, which it sometimes reveals and sometimes does not, sometimes happily, sometimes unhappily" (Raleigh 72). Life, to all of them, becomes a dream of pain.

In the beginning of the play, Mary just comes back after a cure in the sanatorium for her drug addiction. Her return is a hope for the family: she is expected to have the ability to abandon old habit. But the inner struggle is still going on in Mary. She acts like a fighter who has been battling with herself in two roles because of her inability to quit the drug addiction: those of relaxed self-confidence and of nervousness. She pretends to look well in the eyes of her family members. The tension between the two roles is shown in the stage directions:

> *Her first reaction is one of relief. She appears to relax. She sinks*
> *down in one of the wicker armchairs at rear of table and leans her head*
> *back, closing her eyes. But suddenly she grows terribly tense again.*
> *Her eyes open and she strains forward, seized by a fit of nervous panic.*
> *She begins a desperate battle with herself. Her long fingers, warped*
> *and knotted by rheumatism, drum on the arms of the chair, driven by an*
> *insistent life of their own, without her consent (italics original). (1257)*

Out of the men's expectation, she does not get rid of her old habit; instead, she indulges herself into it more seriously. In fact, she is reluctant to face an intense hatred of the present and its morbid, inescapable reality. Facing her present life, she is really unhappy. What she desires is to seek solace from the shocks of life in nostalgic memories. For Mary, morphine is the best key to lock the past. Intoxicated in it, she says: "It kills the pain. You go back until at last you are beyond its reach. Only the past when you were happy is real" (1283). The pain Mary speaks of is in her crippled hands, her failed dreams to be a pianist or a nun, but "even more it is in her crippled, guilt soul" (Brustein, in Bloom 27). Mary has betrayed all her hopes and dreams. Even her marriage is a betrayal. She tells her husband: "But I must confess, James, although I couldn't help loving you, I would never have married you if I'd known you drank so much" (1288). Moreover, she desires a real home in which "one is never lonely" (1268). She complains to her husband about his niggardliness: "He thinks money spent on a home is money wasted. He's lived too much in hotels. Never the best hotels, of course. Second-rate hotels. He doesn't understand a home. He doesn't feel at home in it. And yet, he wants a home. He's even proud of having this shabby place" (1263). The home now Mary lives in is quite different from the home Mary's father sets for her where she enjoys the minor social triumphs she experienced as a young girl and the munificence that her father provided. Obviously, she would have difficulties adjusting to her actor-husband's life. For her difficulty, she creates herself a world of drug addict because of her inefficiency at running a household and raising children. Being an unsuccessful wife and mother, she keeps "her subsequent retreat into an illusionary world may have been forms of revenge. Detesting alcohol, which brought her beloved father to an untimely end, she takes the morphine route, wallowing in self-pity for the failures of her life" (Floyd 541).

In terms of "the failures of her life," Mary could be viewed as both an innocent victim and a guilty victimizer. As a victim, she is spoiled by her father, and when only eighteen, she becomes the wife of a touring actor. She is too young to face a difficult transition. After Edmund's birth, she becomes addicted to morphine because her husband hires a cheap doctor in his miserliness. On the other hand, she is a victimizer and should be partly responsible for her present condition. She vacillates between love and hate. As Edmund points out:

It's pretty horrible to see her the way she must be now. (*with bittermisery*) The hardest thing to take is the blank wall she builds around

her. Or it's more like a bank of fog in which she hides and loses

herself. Deliberately, that's the hell of it! You know something in her

does it deliberately—to get beyond our reach, to be rid of us, to forget

we're alive! It's as if, in spite of loving us, she hated us! (1301)

That Mary loves her husband and children admits no question. However, in a larger sense, love has disturbed her spirit and violated her desire to retain her purity.

Love has led her into a world where she was not and never could be ready. Her love for her younger son is more than her first son and her husband, who has spent money to help her quit the drug addiction. Mary gives up helping herself; instead, she accepts the illusive pleasure that morphine provides. In so doing, the three men in the family feel betrayed. Their hopes of the past two months, when they have confidence in her ability to resist the drug temptation, are totally shattered. Mary is " selfish, vindictive, vengeful, and irresponsible" (Floyd 542).

Actually, Mary has sensed what her failure life has imposed on her. She says: "None of us can help the things life has done to us. They're done before you realize it, and once they're done they make you do other things until at last everything comes between you and what you'd like to be, and you've lost your true self forever" (1262).

Facing the failure, Mary chooses two methods. One is to escape from it, to ignore it. She is subjected to a number of illusions and past memories which could give her temporary harmony and help her "remember only the happy part of the past" (1288). The other is to search for those happy memories she has lost for so long rather than the "true self" she mentions above. According to Travis Bogard, Mary is searching for "a self that does not exit. Repeatedly she remarks that she cannot find her glasses and therefore cannot see to fix her hair. In other words, she cannot see what she is" (67). Indeed, Mary "cannot see what she is" because she is blind to see through her "true self." By the power of drugs, she turns to look for the lost self, "the image has more power over her than any of the difficulties of her present life" (Orr, in Bloom 119). Triumphantly, she reminisces: "I had two dreams. To be a nun, that was the more beautiful one. To become a concert pianist, that was the other" (1283). But the dreams in her girlhood "are dreams of escape which affect her as the morphine does by pulling her from the present, from the house, from the irony of Tyrone's buying property without providing a home, and from her indifference that is like hatred of her family" (Bogard 67). Mary's attitude denies any possibilities for a change toward a new life, a change not only for herself but for her husband and her children.

When the three men around Mary are confronted with the undeniable evidence of Mary's relapse, they turn to alcohol in their disappointment. Then, the family's predicament is reiterated: they use Mary's relapse as an excuse to drink; whereas she uses their indifference as an excuse for her relapse. Like Mary, James Tyrone is doomed to an endless life of regret for something lost in the past. His stinginess and his career as an actor are related to the misery of his wife and children. His miserliness has caused Mary's drug addiction, because he hires a cheap quack doctor who first takes her to it; his inability to provide his wife a real home as she wishes, because he is always on the road, has increased her suffering and the sense of loss. His niggardliness is also the source of Edmund's resentment and recrimination, since he decides to send Edmund to a cheap sanatorium for his tuberculosis treatment instead of an expensive one. For James Tyrone, his thrift is resulted from the fear of the poverty-stricken past. Facing Edmund's question about his tightfistedness, he defends himself by unlocking his bitter memories:

> There was no damned romance in our poverty. Twice we were evicted
> from the miserable hovel we called home, with my mother's few sticks of
> furniture thrown out in the street, and my mother and sisters crying. I
> cried, too, though I tried hard not to, because I was the man of the family.
> At ten years old! There was no more school for me. I worked twelve
> hours a day in a machine shop, learning to make files. A dirty barn of a
> place where rain dripped through the roof, where you roasted in summer,
> and there was no stove in winter, and your hands got numb with cold,
> where the only light came through two small filthy windows, so on grey
> days I'd have to sit bent over with my eyes almost touching the files in
> order to see! . . . It was in those days I learned to be a miser. A dollar
> was worth so much then. And once you've learned a lesson, it's hard to
> unlearn it. You have to look for bargains. If I took this state farm
> sanatorium for a good bargain, you'll have to forgive me. (1306)

The emphasis on thrift presents that he is influenced very deeply by his poverty in the past. It also points out that he has never come to learn a lesson from his poverty and to understand the value of money; that is, kinship is more important than money itself. And at "different stages in the life of the family, its two tragic figures, Edmund and Mary have suffered immeasurably from his meanness and miscalcul-ation" (Orr 120). That is, these two are sacrificed to his fear of poverty-stricken past, to his need for secure wealth which denies him in his childhood. Like a lugged bear, he becomes a target for all of his family's resentment. Even so, he honors the chains of the home more than any other one in this family. He loves them but he is often driven toward hatred. He also lives in pain of the life as Mary does. There-fore, he turns from it to the local barroom; he buys lands in order to get security he cannot find in his past experience; he drinks to dope his mind to the point of forget-fulness.

The second Tyrone man around Mary is Edmund, who deals with his own lost innocence and his present tuberculosis state, and who "is attracted by this oblivion —seeing the fog as blotting out the real, removing him from the social context which is the source of his pain" (Bigsby, in Bloom 128). He says: "Everything loo-ked and sounded unreal. Nothing was what it is. That's what I wanted—to be alone with myself in another world where truth is untrue and life can hide from itself" (1297). Like his mother, he loves the fog because it protects him from truth and re-ality. But he is more romantic than his mother, he goes forward to search for the oblivion in the fog and at the same time he desires the oblivion of death. He utters:

> The fog and the sea seemed part of each other. It was like walking on
>
> the bottom of the sea. As if I had drowned long ago. As if I was a
>
> ghost belonging to the fog, and the fog was the ghost of the sea. It felt
>
> damned peaceful to be nothing more than a ghost within a ghost. (1297)

Edmund has experienced such peaceful feeling at sea, and now it is only a memory. Escape from his present reality seems unattainable so he would like to for-get in alcohol. Unfortunately, drinking does not allow him to forget, let alone es-cape from the present reality. Everything in the course of the day, "has reinforced the sense that it is impossible for this family to forget, and that intoxication exacer-bates the problem" (Bloom, in Martine 171). Certainly, through the picture of the alcoholic, Edmund constantly seeks to escape his problems but the ending he confronts is always drunken in the endless depression.

The third man around Mary is Jamie, who is affected by Edmund's existence, since his little brother's literary talents fill him with envy and a sense of failure; even worse, his mother's drug addiction has made him lose faith in his own capacity. He is "both the creator and destroyer of his brother" (Bogard 77). He reminds Edmund that it is he who takes him to the poetic world and gives him the idea of being a writer. He gives him a creative and rich life. But he also takes his brother into a destroyed world where he deliberately sets him an example of cynicism and dissipated self-destruction. Jamie confesses in front of his brother:

> My putting you wise so you'd learn from my mistakes. Believed that
> myself at times, but it's a fake. Made my mistakes look good. Made
> getting drunk romantic. Made whores fascinating vampires instead of
> poor, stupid, diseased slobs they really are. Made fun of work as
> sucker's game. Never wanted you succeed and make me look even
> worse by comparison. Wanted you to fail. Always jealous of you.
> Mama's baby, Papa's pet! (1316)

Jamie's purgative confession of his love-hate feelings towards his brother is really a confession of his own self-loathing. Loving and hating his brother, Jamie always stays at the past moment that he is loved less by his parents. With the same feeling, he returns to the days before he knows his mother is a drug addict, a big hurt which has driven him to drink and deserted his own life. He recalls: "Caught her in the act with a hypo. Christ, I'd never dreamed before that any women but whores took dope!" (1314). It is obvious that Jamie is besieged in the horrible scene in the past and he cannot stand out from it until now. Like the other family members, he takes and remembers regarding things past. Although they are devastated by the tragic events of their history, they "locate their ideals in the past and experience them as forever beyond their reach" (Porter 109). And at the same time, "all of them revolve around Mary, locating their own hopes for the future in her ability to remain abstemious—a hope which proves doomed" (Porter 109).

Within the addictive family, denial is clearly a prominent behavioral trait which is operative for all the Tyrone men. They deny responsibility for their own lives; however, all three are lost, frustrated, isolated in a world of illusion and self-deception. They have different capacities for denial, and "these differences are consistent with each character's philosophical stance: Edmund is the romantic idealist; Jamie is the cynical realist; and Tyrone is the resigned pragmatist" (Bloom, in Martine 164). However, in common, they are searching for the past, using it "to define the present, but because all the family are speaking, it is not one selected past, but a range of past experiences now relived and altering the present" (Williams 36). Definitely, they are bothered by the ramification of time—the past memories and the present unhappiness, which are the reality of the Tyrones' lives. They are unable to escape the crushing "burden of Time" (1297) no matter the past or the present. The situation they are facing is best defined by Mary when she denies the possibility of forgetting the past. She says, "The past is the present, isn't it? It's the future, too. We all try to lie out of that but life won't let us" (1275). Mary's words signify that the family, on the one hand, is enslaved by Time, and it seems to be intensified by their intoxication. On the other hand, the words are related to Fate, which is in the repeated circles, in the inescapable repetitions, in the power of the past over the present and over the past.

The Tyrones are haunted by the past since there is nowhere to go; there is no escape. Morphine and alcohol "cannot protect them from the emptiness of their lives; these only intensify the feelings of hopelessness, and keep them trapped in circles of behavior and interaction that ultimately leave them all alone" (Bloom, in Martine 176). In the last moments of the play, by the presence of Mary, she speaks while the men look at her in horror: "That was in the winter of senior year. Then in the spring something happened to me. Yes, I remember. I fell in love with James Tyrone and was so happy for a time" (1322). Mary has withdrawn into the dream world of a past where she reenacts the dreams of her youth, oblivious of her surroundings. Meanwhile, her regression makes the three drunken men around her unable to attain oblivion, unable to forget where and who they are. Mary's quest is for a self lost in the past, a hope also lost in the past, and a goalless search for salvation never to be attained. It embodies the sufferings of the four miserable human beings and reestablishes another relentless beginning for all of them.

Works Cited

Bigsby, C. W. E. "The Retreat behind Language." In Bloom, 125-31.

Bloom, Harold. *Eugene O'Neill's Long Day's Journey into Night.* New York: Chelsea House, 1987.

Bloom, Steven F. "Empty Bottles, Empty Dreams: O'Neill's Use of Drinking and Alcoholism in *Long Day's Journey Into Night." Essays on Eugene O'Neill.* Ed. James J. Martine. Boston: G. K. Hall, 1984.

Bogard, Travis. "The Door and the Mirror." In Bloom, 61-81.

Brustein, Robert. "The Theatre of Revolt." In Bloom, 21-33.

Floyd, Virginia. *The Plays of Eugene O'Neill.* New York: Frederick Ungar, 1985.

O'Neill, Eugene. "*Long Day's Journey into Night." The Norton Anthology of American Literature.* 2nd ed. Vol. 2. Ed. Nina Baym, etl. New York: Norton, 1985.

Orr, John. "Eugene O'Neill: The Life Remembered." In Bloom, 115-24.

Porter, Laurin R. "Modern and Postmodern Wastelands: *Long Day's Journey Into Night and Shepard's Buried Child." The Eugene O'Neill Review* 17.1-2 (1993): 106-9.

Raleigh, John Henry. "Communal, Familial, and Personal Memories in O'Neill's *Long Day's Journey Into Night." Modern Drama* 31.1 (1988): 63-72.

Williams, Raymond. "*Long Day's Journey into Night*: Eugene O'Neill." In Bloom, 35-49.

Utopian Visions of *Herland*

盧淑薰
Shu-shiun Lu

國防醫學院
人文及社會科學科講師

摘　　要

加入女性主義觀點的女性烏托邦〈她鄉〉添補了傳統烏托邦之不足，本文旨在探討 Charlotte Perkins Gilman 勾勒之女性烏托邦之女性願景。

The Norman and comfortable state of being is that when
The two live in harmony together, spiritually cooperating.
…It is when this fusion takes place that the mind is fully
fertilized and uses all its faculties.

Virginia Woolf *A Room of One's Own*

The claims of 'biology is destiny', often used in the past
by misogynists to exclude women, are here accepted and
transformed into the definition of women as truly different and inherently superior to men.

Nan Bowman Albinski
Women's Utopias in British and American Fiction

In the beginning of the 20th century, Charlotte Perkins Gilman provided us a
novel, *Herland*, of an ideal society composed, governed and proliferated all by

women. Because, for a long time, having been discriminated and treated with injustice, women yearned for freedom from fear and patriarchy. Elimination of discrimination and emancipation of women were purposes of women's movement. Therefore, feminists traveled into realm of utopia. Gilman's *Herland* presents a fantasy world of women utopia and depicts her utopian visions and strategy.

In the Greek word "utopia" created by Thomas More from two Greek words—eutopos(good place) and outopos(no place),"u" means negative, "topia" means place. So "utopia" means nonexistent land of perfect society. The idea of Utopia is deeply influenced by the Judeo-Christian and Hellenic ancient myths beliefs. According to Frank E. Manuel and Frotzie P. Manuel (17). Paradise and Promised Land are great longings of Christian ideal. Also Plato's Republic evinces his ideal commonwealth of peace and harmony (Kumar 37).

It seems that Thomas More's *Utopia* states the genre of utopia More seems to have "effectively marked out the field of utopia for the next five hundred years" (Kumar 26). Male utopias follow More's steps to portray ideal countries of well-ordered governmental institutions and economical policy. Furthermore, Sargent explains it as follows:

> Utopia may be used as a general term covering all the various classes of utopia literature. Eutopia—although the word has unfortunately fallen out of favor—or the positive utopia refers to presentations of good places. Dystopia or the negative utopia refers to presentations of bad places. The satirical utopia refers to works where the satire is the focus of the work.(xi)

Otherwise, with the same goals of Woman's movement, women writers of eutopia require as delineated by Albinski as follows:

> Rather than silence on marriage and the family, American women suggest a spectrum of equalizing reforms: they wish to rewrite the marriage service and eliminate the double standard of morality, and advocate the sharing (or automation) of domestic tasks. (44)

Also Giovanna Pexxuoli protects that female sexuality merely serves a process channeled for procreation and chauvinism (40). Feminists, with the raising of woman's self-consciousness, refuse to be treated as the "other" in male utopias. Even Gilman, in *Herland*, carrys out a wonderland to make men absent instead of the absence of women in male utopias. Children—girls in *Herland* have no fathers and they are born by mothers only.

In our society, fathers are always rebuked for reducing their importance to giving birth only. In *Herland*, the fantastic parthenogenesis—virgin birth to procreate makes father's missing. The only mission of giving birth of fathers, therefore, doesn't exist. The high tech. of cloning may soon fulfill the dream of Gilman. This ideal is vividly depicted in conversation between Herlanders male intruders:

> "No," she answered quietly. "There are no men in this country. There has not been a man among us for two thousand years."
>
> "But--the people—the children," he protested, not believing her at the least, but not wishing to say so.
>
> "Oh yes," she smiled." I do not wonder you are puzzled. We are mothers—all of us but there are not fathers. We thought you would ask about that long ago—why have you not?" Her look was as frankly kind as always, her tone quite simple.
>
> "Will you excuse us all," he said, "if we admit that we find it hard to believe? There is no such—possibility—in the rest of the world."
>
> "Have you no kind of life where it is possible?" asked Zava.
>
> "Why, yes—some low forms, of course."
>
> "How low—or how high, rather?"
>
> "Well—there are some rather high forms of insect life in which it occurs.

Parthenogenesis, we call it—that means virgin birth." (45)

And it is common to the matriarchal utopias, there are wars in the distant past which have killed all the men, leaving women to control their own destinies. Herlanders make the country a unit and "they themselves [are] a unit" (79) and "they habitually [consider] and [carry] out plans for improvement which might cover centuries" (79).

According to Hester Eisenstein's observation, there are three options of feminist theory:

> First there is the option of agreeing to compete in the male-defined world
> of politics on its own terms, in the manner of Margaret Thatcher. Second,
> there is the option of withdrawing from that world, out of pessimism as
> to its essentially patriarchal nature, creating instead an otherworld of fe-
> male retreat···Finally, there is the option of entering the world and at-
> tempting to change it, in the image of the woman centred values at the
> core of feminism.(144)

Herland belongs to the second option to join the separatist group. The woman
country locates in an isolated and quarantined space—" [o]ut of that dark green sea
of crowding forest this high-standing spur rose steeply. It ran back on either side,
apparently, to the far-off white-crowned peaks in the distance, themselves probably
inaccessible"(10). And the nation of women is set in a remote and hidden place with
"icy ridge at the back end—'[i]t's a pretty enterprising savage who would manage
to get into it,' Jeff said" (10). In the distant wonderland, a matriarchal society fulfills
the highest optimism about achieving utopia. So when intruders of *Herland* is leaving Herlanders require them:

> We are unwilling to expose our country to free communication with the rest
> of the world—as yet. If Ellador comes back, and we approve her report, it
> may be done later—but not yet. (145)

In this separatist utopia, women can escape patriarchy and subordination to build a
country of imagination which composed of emancipated women.

Economic independence is the surest prescription of women's emancipation.
Successful business women and woman engineers are admired. In some female utopian works, writers "put the women to work in colleges, as students and professors,
as lawyers judges and jurors" (Albinski, 61). Women's work is valued and women
have freedom with openness to choose their work in female utopian works.

In *Herland*, they have fantastic architects to cultivate the land like a large park
and utilize every inch of the land ecologically. It is indicated by the narration "a land
in a state of perfect cultivation, where even the forests looked as if they were cared

for; a land that looked like and enormous park, only it was even more evidently an enormous garden" (11). It is amazing that "[p]hysiology, hygiene, sanitation, physical culture—all that line of work had been perfected long since" (71). They should have many high technological scientists and knowledgeable medical women. So "[s]ickness was almost wholly unknown among them, so that a previously high development in what we call the 'science of medicine' had become practically a lost art. They were a clean-bred, vigorous lot, having the best of care, the most perfect living conditions always" (71).

The intelligent women all dedicate themselves to the country and they don't have limitation of hopes and ambitions of an individual life. Therefore, "they habitually [consider] and [carry] out plans for improvement which might cover centuries"(79). They offer suggestions for economic self-help, carry out successful programs to increase public health through better housing and nutrition.

Herlanders are wise, strong and gentle with courage to overcome problems of economy, education, and agriculture. They love each other with feeling of siblings to establish a civilized society without women's subordinate position, patriarchal hierarchy, and even oppression.

Although Herlanders' parthenogenesis, with high speed of technological progress, will come true someday in the future, the idea of androgyny and extinction of men is still hard to accept in our society. Adrienne Rich imagines the situation with a question and an answer: "Could you imagine a world of women only,···Absently, wearily, I answered: Yes" (66). Otherwise, could you imagine a world of men only?

Also the idea of retreat and running away from men to escape to an isolated place is defective. After all, women should confront the oppressions and overthrow them. They are necessities during the struggle against patriarchal power and institutions. Gilman's awakening utopian visions and strategies proclaim women's hardship and helplessness.

Works Cited

Albinski, Nan Bowman. *Women's Utipias in Britsh and American Fiction*. London: Routledge, 1988.

Eisenstein, Hester. *Contemporary Feminist Thought*. London, 1984.

Gilman, Charlotte Perkins. Herland. 1915. New York: Pantheon Books P, 19791

Kumar, Krishan. *Concepts in the Social Sciences: Utopianism*. Buckingham,UK: Open UP, 1991.

Manuel, Frank E. and Fritzie P. Manuel. "Introduction: The Utopian Propensity" *Utopian Thought in the Western World*. Cambridge: the Berknap P, 1979, 93-114.

Pexxuoli, Gilvanna. "Prisoner in Utopia." *Theory and Practice of Feminist Literary Criticism*. Eds. Gabriela Mora and Karen S. Van Hooft. Ypsilanti, MI: Bilingula, 1982. 36-43.

Rich, Adrienne. "Natural Resources." The Dream of a Common Language: Poems1974-1977. London: W.W.Norton & Company, Inc., 1978. 60-67.

Sargent, Lyman Tower. Annotated Bibliography, 1st edn.

Woolf, Virginia. *A Room of One's Own*. Ed. Morag Shiach. Oxford: Oxford UP, 1992.